The Italian American Experience

THE ITALIANS OF NEWARK
A COMMUNITY STUDY

Charles W[esley] Churchill

ARNO PRESS
A New York Times Company
New York — 1975

Reprint Edition 1975 by Arno Press Inc.

Copyright © 1975 by Charles W. Churchill

Reprinted by permission of Charles W. Churchill

The Italian American Experience
ISBN for complete set: 0-405-06390-3
See last pages of this volume for titles.

Publisher's Note: This thesis was reprinted
from the best available copy.

Manufactured in the United States of America

Library of Congress Cataloging in Publication Data

Churchill, Charles Wesley, 1911–
    The Italians of Newark.

    (The Italian American experience)
    Reprint of the author's thesis, New York
University, 1942.
    Bibliography: p.
    1. Italian Americans—New Jersey—Newark.
2. Newark, N. J.—Social conditions. I. Title.
II. Series.
F144.N6C5 1975   917.49'32'0651   74-17922
ISBN 0-405-06395-4

T H E   I T A L I A N S   O F   N E W A R K

A COMMUNITY STUDY

By

Charles W. Churchill

SUBMITTED IN PARTIAL FULFILLMENT
OF THE REQUIREMENTS FOR THE DEGREE OF
DOCTOR OF PHILOSOPHY

NEW YORK UNIVERSITY

1942

PREFACE

Initial Field work on this book was concentrated on securing answers to an interview schedule from a representative group of Italians. In all about 700 Italians were interviewed of which approximately one-half were born in Italy. The interview schedule is reproduced in the appendix. Estimates of the Italian population were garnered from the United States Census of 1930 as modified by estimates of various Italian leaders plus the well-known downward trend of population. The final estimate of Italians in Newark of all generations was between 70,000 and 80,000. The sample then represents about 1% of the total and a somewhat larger percentage of the adults. Basic figures for the wards of the city were used as a basis for a number of interviews to be taken in the different sections of the city. Interviewers were instructed to get respondents up to the estimated number required in each Ward. Their instructions were to take not more than one interview to a block except in a heavily congested Italian district. It is believed that the sample is as representative as is possible.[1] The questionnaire was pretested by 100 interviews on the basis of which minor corrections were made. Reference to definite proportions throughout the book are based on this questionnaire which was asked of some 5,000 residents of New Jersey.

As it was, realizing that Italians were a difficult population to interview because of their suspicions of the purpose of the interviewers,

[1] See appendix for a ward analysis of interviews as well as a chart of provinces of origin.

only Italian speaking interviewers were used. During the course of the
interviewing which covered a period from March, 1938, to August, 1939,
six Italian interviewers did field work. All of them were trained as
carefully as possible in the technics of interviewing before being
permitted into the field and their early interviews were discarded in
order to weed out early istakes.

Interviewers were required to memorize the schedule and carried
with them only a skeleton interview in which to mark answers.

Interviewers themselves were men from low income families; 3 were
born in America and 3 were Italian born. One was a North Italian and
the remainder were South Italians. They were instructed to use Italian
instead of English in interviewing first generati n Italians.

Checking studies on a modified interview schedule were made in
Trenton and Paterson. Practically the same results were achieved in
these centers, although the samples were considerably smaller.
Tabulation of the results was included in this study.

The limitations of the questionnaire technic being fully recognized,
a number of other standard technics were used. The early history of
each group was constructed from available source material such as newspapers, books and pamphlets. The memories of old residents were tapped
to complete the picture. Organizations of all kinds were visited and
functions of each group attended. Records of various courts and city
departments were analyzed by etnnic groups.

The purpose of this study, which was sponsored by the Goodwill
Commission of the State of New Jersey and organized as a unit of the
New Jersey Writers' Project, was to present a picture of Italian

community life in order that the average citizen might gain an understanding of his Italian fellow-citizen. The purpose was not to glorify the Italian by making a survey of his good points alone but to analyze the forces and institutions whic have made the Italian comnunity what it is. There are some phases of the Italian population which are disturbing. However, it is not felt that Italians should be blamed for their deficiencies, which where they existed were fully as much the fault of the American population. At any rate, it is hoped that the reader will realize the Italian population of Newark is a part of the stream of history and, as such, has almost inevitably resulted in the kind of group which it is.

A number of Italian leaders have been kind enough to lend assistance to the project. Among these are Messrs. Joseph Di Deo, Manager of the Columbus Hospital; Peter Baldasa, President of the Italian C tholic Union; John J. Sileo, Editor of the Italian Tribune; Olindo Marzulli, publisher of The Italian American; Francesco Palleria, Grand Venerable of the Sons of Italy; Professor Caspare Nicotri; Dr. C.G. Berardinelli; Rudolph Colamedici, photographer; Father Justice of Immaculate Conception Roman Catholic Church; Father Viccaro of Mt. Carmel Roman Catholic Church; Alfred di Adeo, president of the Abruzzese Society; former Judge Mancusso Ungaro; and Mr. Frank Cozzolino. Cooperation was secured from Mayor Meyer C. Ellenstein and Commissioners Pierce R. Franklin, Vincent J. Murphy, and Joseph _. Byrne; Judge Felix Forlenso of the Essex County Juvenile and Domestic Relations Court helped in permitting use of court records. Trade union data was secured from Mr. Thomas Gallanoz, business agent of Local 27 of the International

Fur and Leather Workers Union and Mr. James Leonardi, business agent
of Local 140. For the International Ladies Garment Workers Union,
Mr. Antonio Crevello, Manager of Local 144 was very helpful. Secretary-
Treasurer Naiman of the Amalgamated Clothing Workers contributed information on his union as well as Mr. Gerard Chiari, of Local 195.
Mr. Frazer L. Holzloner of the Bricklayers and Plasterers Union Local 16
was a source of information. There are many others too numerous to
mention who have given of their time to add to the authenticity of the
picture. Their aid is gratefully acknowledged.

C.N.C.

March 30, 1942

TABLE OF CONTENTS

VI. At Work

Tradesmen, Laborers, Professions, Unemployment, Public
Employment, Trade Unions -- The Needle Trades, Leather and Fur,
Accomodation to Other National Groups.

VII. Family Life

The Central Place of the Family in Italian Social Organization
in Italy -- The Role and Status of Women, The Role and Status
of Men, The Role and Status of Children, The Role and Status
of Godparents; The Influence of the Second Generation -- Children
of Two Cultures, Conflict with Parents, Family Difficulties,
Declining Size of Family.

VIII. Religion and The Church

Background in Italy, Early Difficulties in Newark -- Language,
Funds; The First Mission, St. Philip Neri, Our Lady of Mt. Carmel,
St. Lucy's, St. Rocco's, Church of the Immaculate Conception,
Protestant Churches -- Olivet Chapel, The First Italian Baptist
Church, The First Italian Presbyterian Church; Influence of
the Church.

IX. Political Life

As a Prestige Factor, Early Participation in Newark, Effect of
Regionalism, Conflict with Irish and Germans, The Republican
Party, Role of the Press, Political Office, Political Attitudes --
Local, National, International.

CHAPTER I

ORIGINS AND BACKGROUNDS IN ITALY OF AMERICAN IMMIGRANTS[1]

Italy is no exception to the general rule that understanding of a people must be based on knowledge of the environmental forces that have affected them. Inasmuch as Italian-Americans are primarily products of pre-war Italy, the discussion will be confined to the pre-fascist physical and social background. It is obvious, however, that fascist influences have been at work on the American of Italian extraction and this influence is discussed in later chapters.

It is not possible to speak of Italians as a unified group. Just as this country has its New Englanders, Southerners, Westerners and other sectional groups, so in Italy there are four fairly well defined areas, each with individual characteristics: a northern, industrial area comprising the old provinces of Piedmont (Piemonte), Lombardy (Lombardia), Venice (Veneto), Liguria, and Emilia; the central provinces, composed of Tuscany (Toscana), the Marches (Marche), Umbria, Lazio, Abruzzi and Molise; the southern part of the peninsula, from which came the greatest Italian migration to the United States, composed of Campania, Le Puglie, Basilicata and Calabria; and the islands of

[1]This chapter draws heavily on Robert Foerster, Italian Emigration of Our Times, (Cambridge: Harvard University Press, 1924). No better sources were found than this excellent definitive work of the Italian waves of migration to points all over the world.

Sicily (Sicilia) and Sardinia (Sardegna).

But subdivision goes much further than these four primary groups. Each province in South Italy, for example, has its own dialect and within each province, towns are little autonomous (sociological) units. Italian immigrants point out that whereas in this country each town and city looks much like another; in Italy each little town has its own distinguishing characteristics from the style of architecture to the customs of the people.

Basically the large Italian emigration to America had its roots in a widespread poverty resulting from several major circumstances: the late unification of Italy, heavy taxation, absentee landlordism, primitive education, lack of natural resources, limited food supply and loss of land by peasants to the great landowners.

Italy did not achieve unification until 1870, when the combined efforts of Cavour, Mazzini and Garibaldi brought the peninsula under the House of Savoy. The ability of Victor Emmanuel II, then King of Sardinia and Piedmont, to accept limitations set upon a constitutional monarch made it possible to unite all elements in the movement under one person.

By the 1815 Treaty of Vienna, Italy was partitioned into a number of small and often warring states dominated by Austria or France. During the great revolutionary movement of 1848 Charles Albert of the House of Savoy, King of Sardinia, entered into a fight for liberation from Austria. His two-year struggle ended in a failure, but Italians

[2]See Kent Greenfield, Economics and Liberalism in the Risorgimento (Baltimore: The Johns Hopkins Press, 1934), for an account of the background of the revolution of 1848.

favoring unification came to feel that his relatively progressive little kingdom had forged rulers who would one day wrest Italy from the invader. Charles Albert, forced to abdicate by his defeat, was succeeded by his son, Victor Emmanuel II. Victor's retention of the charter which his father had granted to the people won him wide popularity, and Italy continued to look to his House for leadership.

Cavour, appointed in 1852 as Victor Emmanuel's prime minister, plotted to have an Italian Confederation nominally led by the Pope but actually under the House of Savoy. To this end he encouraged trouble between Napoleon III and Austria, but failed to achieve his purpose. He then changed his plan to aim at a unified kingdom under Victor Emmanuel. All Italy was now seething with revolt. The only provinces which could not join the movement were Venice and Rome, due to the presence of foreign troops.

The ten-year unification process began in 1859 when the northern states (except Venesia) revolted and quickly united with Sardinia. Southern Italy, roused by the famous maren of Garibaldi, rallied to his banner. One by one the remaining states voted to join the new kingdom. The goal was reached in 1870 when, over the objections of the Pope, Rome capitulated and the Kingdom of Italy became a reality.

The new kingdom inherited the woes of centuries of civil war and foreign invasion. South Italy was almost one unrelieved mass of illiteracy, while in the north only a small beginning had been made in education.

The ancient heritage of sectionalism was one of the great problems facing the new nation. After the first great wave of enthusiasm, deputies fell back to their provincial perspective, fostering measures to benefit their own localities rather than the kingdom as a whole.

Although favoring decentralization, Cavour modeled the administration on the French system, with the central government empowered to intervene at almost any point in local functions. Old territories were merged into artificial provinces, each headed by an official whom the king appointed with little regard for local issues. Strangely enough the judiciary was extremely decentralized, so it exercised little control over the centralized administration.

There were local elective offices, but education requirements so restricted the suffrage that only $2\frac{1}{2}$ percent of the population voted. In 1882 voting was extended to all who could read and write or pass examinations on subjects compulsory in the local school system. Officials, college graduates, military heroes and those who paid taxes of 20 lire or more, or large rents, also were granted the suffrage.

A combination of legitimate and illegitimate governmental expenses involved in building a new nation made Italy one of the most heavily taxed nations of Europe. As high as 54 percent of the taxes were paid by the poorest classes. In addition, Italy had a high protective tariff, which added to the burden of the poor. Delivet reckoned that Italy gathered from its poor 17 percent of income, while France took 12 percent, Germany 8 percent and England 6 percent. De Foville, on the other hand, estimated taxation at 30 percent of income, most of it gathered from the poor.[3] Salt and tobacco were

[3]Bolton King and Thomas Okey, Italy Today (New York: Charles Scribner and Sons, 1913), p. 137-141.

monopolies of the government, and both were heavily taxed. Sicily,
a large producer of salt, because of taxes had to pay four cents a
pound, while untaxed it would have been worth two cents for ten pounds.
Other heavily taxed articles were wheat, flour, bread and macaroni. Not
only was there a tariff on imported products, but each little section
added its bit by assessing duties. Everywhere were little custom houses,
and each had its guards search all vehicles for dutiable items.
Practically everything had a duty. Rents too were higher because of
taxation. Many were the ways of attempting to avoid duties, and the
whole country was tax-evasion conscious.

Francis Clark, when discussing the problem of why Italians
emigrated, wrote "the reason may be summed up in two words, namely:
'poverty and taxes'."[4] Professor Villari says, "it is progressive
taxation, topsy turvy, and the less a man has, the more he pays."[5]

Contrary to the American theory of taxation in accordance with
ability to pay,[6] Italy exacted relatively high taxes from the poor.
Consequently, all necessities were taxed and all luxuries excepted. To
add to the unequal burden, the south suffered heavy inequalities in
assessments, the basis of which was inaccurate in conception and
unequal in application. As everything else, tax reform was hard to

[4] Francis Clark, Our Italian Fellow Citizens (Boston: Small Maynard
and Co.), p. 74.

[5] Ibid, p. 82.

[6] Very often more honored in the breach than in the observance

achieve in south Italy. Dairy and draft animals were taxed, but the horses of the aristocracy were exempt.

The two general taxes were the state land tax and that of the local commune. Theoretically the commune tax was not to exceed 50 percent of the state tax but in actuality it was usually higher. The Dazio Consumo or consumers tax imposed a tremendous burden on the poor man as it taxed all food and necessities.[7]

The poor man, moreover, drew little return from his taxes. Public services were badly managed and corrupt. Frequently a specific tax was completely absorbed by wasteful methods of collection.

The north, where the tax system was almost as bad as in the south, achieved reform somewhat earlier. In addition, its higher economic status and the greater variety of taxable goods furnished a broader base. Reforms included elimination of local custom duties and of the tax on farm animals.

Absentee landlordism had its origin in the same phenomenon that occurred in other countries of Europe. Feudal barons originally lived in castles on their holdings. The Bourbons, in order to break the power of the local barons, established in Naples a court which by its gaiety, royal honors and diversions drew the lords away from their estates which they left in charge of either contadini (peasants) or factors. The factors played both ends against the middle and enriched themselves from proprietors as well as tenants. In their short-

[7]A fuller discussion of the tax problem may be found in King and Okey, op. cit., pp. 270-272 and pp. 374-376.

sighted greed they gave the land no rest. Soil exhaustion resulted. In 1901 3/8 of the Basilicatan, 2/5 of the Calabrian and as many as 2/3 of the Sicilian landowners were not living on their estates.[8]

As the average absentee landlord held more land than the resident proprietor, the percentage of land managed by the owners was even smaller than the percentage of persons cultivating their own land.

The situation was much more acute in the south than in the north. Proprietors of rich lands repaired to the large cities, while those of more modest means lived in the provincial capitals.

The aristocracy, following the conventional pattern, was interested only in life of leisure and gaiety in the big cities. The only accepted professions were the military or the church. Balls, hunting, traveling, dress, racing and games were the orbit of their existence.

In Sicily a new enterprising substitute for the landlord proprietors arose, the Gabelloto or great leaseholder. The Gabelloti leased nobles' estates for a period averaging six years. They then sublet to tenants. The terms of the contracts varied in different provinces of the south, but always the Gabelloto received more than his share. He was interested only in extracting as much as he could out of his tenants, abandoning the land as it wore out.[9] In north Italy also absentee landlordism was prevalent, and management of property was left to

[8] Censimento, 1901, V pp. CXXI, 135. For fuller comment see Foerster, op. cit., pp. 70-82.

[9] In some regions there was a pyramiding of leases. A large Gabelloto would sublease to a smaller Gabelloto. This is the usual pattern. Foerster, op. cit., pp. 73-76.

ignorant or unscrupulous people.

In pre-war Italy the lands tended to become more and more concentrated in the hands of a few. When feudalism was abolished, technically in the early 19th century, it appeared for a time that the communes would achieve widespread distribution of land.[10] However, between the machinations of the Bourbons and the landlords and the burden of taxation the little men were squeezed out.

The second great distribution took place with the expropriation of church lands between 1855 and 1873. However, in Sicily, for instance, the lands were leased at higher rentals and reverted to the state if payments were delinquent three months. The result was that the lands fell into the hands of the great proprietors. The same phenomenon occurred throughout south Italy.[11]

To add to the troubles of the peasant, the division of property at the death of the father resulted in fragmentation of land below the amount necessary for successful farming. On the other hand the great estates of the south belonging to the aristocracy tended to remain intact, due to such practices as marrying off only one son and bequeathing no lands to daughters. In 1901 there were actually fewer landed proprietors in Basilicata, Calabria and Sicily than in 1882,

[10]Feudalism was abolished in South Italy in 1806 and in Sicily in 1812.

[11]L. Franchetti and S. Sonnino, La Sicilia nol 1876 (2 Vols.,Florence, 1877), i, ca.ii, p.115 and ii, p.290; Inchesta Agraria, IX, pp. 57, 105,114f; Ciolfi, ch. VI, esp. pp. 81-89; Arca, p. 107. Quoted in Foerster, op. cit., p. 65.

indicating the concentration of holdings.[12] In North Italy, on the other hand, there had been more subdivision of landed estates. In some regions of the north small plots abounded. Though there were many great estates, they did not occupy the dominant position that they did in the south.

The tendency toward centralization of land control was somewhat offset by returning emigrants who with foreign gold proceeded to buy parcels of land from small proprietors or from owners of large estates. No figures are available for the extent of this influence.

After unification the school system was modeled on the German form. Education was the responsibility of each local governmental unit.[13] Although the cities offered fair educational advantages, the small villages suffered from the apathy of the peasant, who saw little use for learning, and the school officials, who feared the social unrest resulting from mass education. Later laws were passed providing that the local communes must have school systems.[14]

In spite of this start, illiteracy remained prevalent. Physical facilities were poor, especially in the country, and teachers were badly paid. The elementary school provided for four or five years of instruction, at most, and some parents withdrew their children even sooner. The next school was the ginnasio, corresponding roughly to the American high school. It covered a period of five years. The liceo, a three-year course, was somewhat less extensive than the

[12] Foerster, op. cit., p. 69

[13] The Minister of Education had nominal control over the schools with an elaborate staff of inspectors, etc. Little money was appropriated, however, and observance of the general laws by the communes was very inefficient.

[14] See Chapter XII in King and Okey, op. cit., for an extensive discussion of education.

American college. Finally there were some of the world's most famous
universities, where excellent educational facilities were available.
However, here were found few people from the lower socio-economic classes.

The difference between education in the north and south is the
result of a long historical process. The north under Austria made some
attempt to improve the schools, but the south under the Bourbons in the
kingdom of the two Sicilies suffered from the educational theories of
Ferdinand II, who believed that the less people knew the less trouble
they were.[15]

The average Italian peasant had perhaps five years of indifferent
schooling, punctuated by considerable absences. 1911 found almost
40 percent of the population of Italy over six years old illiterate.[16]
The lower incidence of illiteracy in north Italy hides the fact that in
this year four of the southern groups; the Abruzzi, Basilicata, Calabria
and Sicily had illiteracy rates of 58, 65, 70 and 58 respectively.[17]
By 1917 Professor Mangano estimated 7,000,000 illiterates but does not
reveal his source.

South Italy, under the thumb of the church and its often poorly
educated priests, was the victim of Roman Catholic opposition to
secular schools, which were not permitted to teach religion. Even in
the north education was poor, limited almost entirely to the elementary schools. Classes were crowded and held only in the winter.

[15]Malcessi and Zanotti-Bianco, p. 83-101, 129-132. Quoted in
Foerster, op. cit., p. 96

[16]Consimente, III, p. 230, Foerster, op. cit., p. 515

[17]Antonio Mangano, Sons of Italy (New York: Missionary Education
Movement, 1917), p. 59.

However, there were some cities which gave adequate courses.

The traditional temporary exodus of northern Italians into other countries of Europe was encouraged by establishing schools to train the emigrants, particularly in industry. Since earnings were brought back into Italy, there was reason enough for encouraging the migrant workers.

Literacy tests in the United States for immigrants stimulated schooling, and there has in Fascist Italy, and even before, been a definite attempt to extend education to south Italy.[18] But, as most emigration occurred in the earlier years of the century, the Italian in America shows little evidence of it.

In physical resources Italy leaves much to be desired as the basis of a modern industrial nation. Bordered on the north and west by the Alps, the top of the boot of Italy is a great basin of the Po River and its tributaries. Rising in the western Alps, the Po flows east and empties into the Adriatic south of Venice. The northern part of the province of Veneto is mountainous, while the other northern provinces are bordered by mountains. Running down the whole length of the peninsula are the Appennine Mountains, extending into the toe and heel. Sicily, too, is largely covered with mountain ranges.

The 5,357 miles of seacoast have since the dawn of the country's history furnished the background for the prominent place of the fishing

[18]Even before the literacy test was adopted in the United States (1917) there were attempts to anticipate this measure. In 1904, 1905, and 1913, action was taken to establish schools in communes from which there was wholesale emigration to the United States. "Rendiconte delle sedute del consiglio dell' Emigrazione tenute nell' anno 1903", Boll. Emig., 1904, No.9, p. 64, and "Rendiconti sommero delle sedute ...nell' anno 1904", Boll. Emig., 1904, No.10, pp. 34-36; cf. Boll. Emig., 1906, No.13, p. 20f, and T. Tittone, Boll. Emig., 1905, No.16, p. 30, and "Proebizione dello sbarco negli State Unite aglu straniere analfabela", Boll. Emig., 1915, Nos.10-12, p. 126. Quoted in Foerster, p. 519.

industry in the Italian economy.

Contrary to its reputation as a land of great fertility, Italy has to struggle with a generally unfavorable physical basis for agriculture. The whole of South Italy and Sicily are deficient in rainfall throughout the summer, which makes it necessary to specialize in crops maturing in the spring. Lack of water makes dairying and grazing a precarious occupation at best. As a corollary, there is a grave lack of natural fertilizers.[19]

One natural resource, water power, Italy has in abundance. Streams are short and drop swiftly from the mountains to the coast, representing unharnessed electric power running into billions of kilowatts. The present administration is taking steps toward utilizing this.

These streams, however, have added to Italy's agricultural problems. Since the deforestation in the eighteenth and nineteenth centuries, the country has experienced numerous landslides. Sometimes whole villages have been buried. Sicily, especially, suffers in this respect. There is considerable evidence that Sicily was once heavily wooded, but the forests have receded steadily. Prior to 1877 the cutting of trees was restricted to the immediate needs of each community. Although the law was widely violated, the removal of restriction gave impetus to deforestration and swift-moving streams carried masses of gravel down from the mountains and deposited it on the fertile plains. Moreover, the streams, unrestrained by forest growth and swollen during the rainy season, broke their banks and flooded the lowlands, creating great

[19]See reports of Inch. Parl., Cf. Risultate dell' inchiesta sulle condizione igienche e sanitarie nei comuni del regno; relazione generale (Rome, 1886), Ch. V. Quoted in Foerster, p. 51.

swamps which withdrew still more of the land from cultivation. The
consequent prevalence of malaria made Italy notorious among European
nations. In recent years the Fascist government has speeded up the
reclamation of these swamps.

There is much discussion amongst historians as to whether there
have been serious climatic changes in Siciliy since classical times,
leaving a much drier climate.[20] The weight of classical allusions
certainly seems to indicate that Sicily, one of the granaries of the
Roman world, had a much more favorable climate then.[21] In recent times
its prosperity has dwindled, and for years prior to mass migration to
America it had been one of the most poverty stricken areas in Europe.

Compared to its natural resources and the status of industrial
development, Italy is undoubtedly heavily overpopulated. In 1936 the
population was about 42½ million, or 138.6 people per square kilometer.
The highest density was in Campania, with 273.8 per square kilometer.
Even under the most modern agricultural conditions it is impossible to
feed the population on any standard of adequacy without extensive
importation, particularly of wheat. Every available inch of terrain
is used for agriculture. Shortage of first class tillable soil has
produced the system of terrace farming up the sides of hills.

The climate is by no means as favorable as is generally supposed.
While it is generally true that the south is warmer than the north, the

[20] See Ellsworth Huntingdon "Climatic Change and Agricultural Exhaustion
as Elements in the Fall of Rome", Quarterly Journal of Economics,
February, 1917, p. 173-208. Quoted in Foerster, op. cit., p. 52-53

[21] Mosso, p. 369-400. Quoted in Foerster, op. cit., p. 53

altitude of much of southern Italy makes it necessary to wear heavy
garments during the winter. Shortage of water in the south has had a
direct effect on the social habits of the Italians. There the rainfall
is little more than half that of New York City and is concentrated
principally in the winter. Drinking water is gathered and sold by
peddlers known as carrettari (carters). One source of supply was the
unmelted snows on the higher slopes.

In north Italy rainfall is greater and climatic conditions are more
generally favorable for agriculture. Moreover, water power available
from the longer rivers has supplied the basis for industrial development
in the north almost exclusively.

Sicily at one time was the chief source of lemons and oranges
brought to America, but since California and Florida developed their fruit
growing, imports from Sicily have declined drastically. There is still,
however, a considerable market in Europe.

One large industry in Sicily is sulphur mining. Before the first
World War it employed 30,000 men and produced almost 500,000 tons of
sulphur a year. There was also an extensive marble industry.

Milan and Genoa are great industrial cities. Milan is the industrial capital, the leading machine producing town. Genoa rivals Naples
as a seaport. The world center for the making of Borsalino hats is in
the north Italy town of Allessandria. Among other manufactured products
are: surgical instruments and fine steel products, locomotives, elec-
trical equipment, especially for use in connection with water power, and
certain fine food products such as olive oil.

Wages compared to American standards were very low. A boiler maker

just before the war earned about $1 a day. Skilled mechanics were
approaching the top at $1.60 a day, while laborers were doing well at
70¢ a day. These figures prevailed in the relatively prosperous
northern parts of the country.[22]

In general, industrial and agricultural conditions, wages, living
conditions and all that forms the physical basis for living decreased
steadily from north to south. The sulphur miners of Sicily felt themselves prosperous at 60¢ a day, while the general average was considerably lower. Quarrying earned for the skilled worker less than
$1 a day.

Women very often earned only half as much as the men. Thus in
cotton mills where the men received 50¢ the women would get as low as
25¢; these rates were for an average ten-hour day. Even so, this was
considerably more than had been paid twenty years earlier. In agriculture before the war laborers did not make 50¢ a day and women less
than half of that. In South Italy laborers received on the average of
35¢, a woman 17 to 18¢. Official figures for the yearly pay of
agricultural laborers in the north ran to about $100 a year, while in
The Marches the average was $50.[23] The south received considerably less.[24]

King and Okey present the following table of agricultural wages
and hours of labor in the chief provinces of Italy for the year 1905.

[22]Clark, op. cit., p. 75-76

[23]Ibid, p. 12

[24]This of course is per person. The family income would depend on
number in family, age and sex.

AGRICULTURAL WAGES AND HOURS OF LABOR
BY PROVINCES IN 1905

1905	AV. HRS. WORKED DAILY	DURA- TION OF MEAL TIMES	AVERAGE DAYS PAY			HIGHEST AND LOWEST EARN- INGS PER MONTH MEN		TOTAL ANNUAL INCOME men
			Men	Women	Boys	Summer	Winter	
Piedmont	10.52	2.07	$ .45	$ .23	$ ...	$17.41	$ 4.16	$106.25
Veneta	9.14	2.07	.34	.21	...	9.25	2.96	77.04
Lombardy	9.44	2.10	.32	...	...	8.59	3.75	70.04
Liburia	10.06	1.40	.39	...	...	13.50	3.12	80.92
Emilia	9.43	1.56	.37	.22	.16	14.00	2.64	74.10
Tuscany	9.57	1.50	.33	...	...	8.35	2.87	73.54
Pomagna	.....	2.07	.40	.23	...	13.85	2.53	85.06
Marches	8.57	2.13	.27	.15	.10	9.85	1.43	52.18
Latium	9.20	2.08	.40	.23	.13	17.50	4.35	95.22
Umbria	9.33	2.02	.34	.19	.13	12.61	1.68	65.39
Abrossi	9.54	2.07	.38	.18	.12	9.35	2.39	83.45
Campania	9.42	2.02	.34	.15	.13	8.50	4.06	80.70
Pullia	8.36	1.31	.33	.14	.11	8.04	3.37	78.56
Basilicata	10.07	2.00	.37	.15	.15	13.00	1.80	84.50
Calabra	9.49	2.11	.36	.12	.16	11.83	4.19	77.85
Sicily	10.03	1.59	.31	.16	.15	8.85	4.50	78.25
Sardinia	9.13	2.17	.35	.15	.15	11.69	5.10	92.25

The average daily wage of male agricultural laborers for all of Italy was $.35. The average number of working days in a year was 225. These figures do not include meals furnished by the employer. Not all districts, however, supply food.

Moreover, the cost of living was not low as might be expected. Francis Clark states that prices were as high as 4¢ a pound for flour before the war, while sugar with the innumerable duties reached as high as 19¢. In spite of this condition, it is true that pre-war prices in Italy were considerably higher for vegetables and somewhat cheaper for meats.[26]

It is small wonder that reports of $2 or more a day in America drew thousands of immigrants. Considering the wage differential and the fact that taxation produced relatively high prices, the wonder is that Italy was not entirely depopulated.

[26]Op. cit., p. 81.

CHAPTER II

PERIOD OF MOVEMENT

Except for a sprinkling on the Atlantic seaboard, colonial and
post-revolutionary America sheltered no Italian immigrants. Between
1820 and 1850, only 4,500 Italians entered.

In 1850, when the census first distinguished residents by nationality, it recorded 3,645 Italians. In the following decade came
8,940 -- an insignificant trickle in the streams of immigrants then
pouring in from Western Europe. By 1860, 10,518 Italians were living
in the United States.[1]

During the next twenty years the number increased progressively.
During the Civil War years and after 1870, 12,206 Italians were dropped
on American shores by the primitive "trans-Atlantic" of the times. By
1870 it was estimated that the American population included 17,157
Italians. The next decade 1871-1880 witnessed a sharp rise to a total
of 55,759 and in the year 1880 -- the year which marked the beginning
of the giant inundations of incoming Italians with which America was
to become increasingly familiar -- 44,230 Italians were still in the
United States. The seeming discrepancy of immigration and total
population is due to the large scale return to Italy.

---

[1]The census figures are open to question in the early censi. It may
be presumed that they rather underestimate the total of Italians in
the United States.

These early sons of Italy, scattered over the strange face of America, have left few records. In the main North Italians, their small numbers permitted them to escape not only the attention of anti-immigrationalists but also the statisticaly observation of governmental authorities.[2] There was no Italian state to extend paternal care. They were a miscellany of workers, traders, vendors of plaster statues and street musicians who came to America in search of permanent settlement-- not easy riches. A few were political refugees, escaping the ire of the Bourbons, such as the legendary Garibaldi, who earned his living and prepared the military campaigns of a later day as a candle-maker on Staten Island.[3]

Two literary reminiscences offer romantic but vague impressions of these isolated Italians. The "Southern Literary Messenger" of December 1842 printed the anonymous "Letters of an Italian Exile." C. Gardini's "Gli Stati Uniti" (Bologna, 1867) relates how 300 Italian miners joyfully walked five miles laden with gifts and fruits, which they laid at the feet of the first Italian woman to grace the state of California.

After 1880 such romantic legends made way for a more realistic evaluation. The new world, hungry for laborers, beckoned to the hard-pressed peoples of the ancient peninsula. And once more legions from Italy marched to all corners of the earth. This time they came not as conquering soldiers or intrepid explorers, but as intelligent although

[2]Giovannai Schiavo in his Italians in America before the Civil War has collected a number of stray records of Italians. The emphasis, how-ever, is on rather prominent individuals. (New York: The Vigo Press,1934).

[3]Ibid. Chap. XII, p. 211-214

illiterate laborers asking for a place to live and a job to perform.
They went not only to the United States but to South America as well, and
in some cases to the countries of Northern Europe, including Finland and
Russia.

Statistics generally tend to congeal such a mighty mass migration,
which Foerster asserts "belongs among the extraordinary movements of
mankind", into frigid charts and appear thereby to rob it of human and
historic connotations. Nevertheless, the table below, based on statistics compiled by the New York Italian Chamber of Commerce, indicate the
significance of this dynamic increase of Italian emigrants. The
figures are for the years indicated and are not cumulative.

EMIGRANTS FROM ITALY BY ANNOUNCED DESTINATION*

YEAR	TOTAL FOR ALL COUNTRIES (including Canada)	UNITED STATES
1880	119,901	5,711
1885	157,193	12,485
1890	215,854	47,952
1895	293,181	37,851
1900	352,782	87,714
1905	726,331	316,569
1910	651,475	262,554
1915	146,019	51,720
1920	614,611	349,042
1925	280,091	29,728

The tide of immigration ebbed and flowed with seismographic
sensitivity to the tremors of world and specifically Italian conditions.
Between 1900 and 1910, years during which American industries enjoyed
an extended boom, 2,104,309 Italians passed through Ellis Island.
Returns to Italy brought the net increase down to 1,345,125. Repatri-
ation, rare in other groups, had marked Italian immigration since its

*New York Italian Chamber of Commerce, 50th anniversary booklet,
"L'Emigrazione I'Italiana dal 1876 al 1925, i sua distribuzione per
gli Stati Uniti."

beginning. It was due to the immigrant's original purpose, failure to adjust himself, or an overwhelming nostalgia for his native country.

The year 1913, eve of the First World War, saw the spiral of Italian immigration achieve its broadest whirl; 1,249,374 Italians sailed towards strange ports, 376,776 of them, the highest total ever reached, coming to America.[4] The end of the war also brought large numbers, fleeing from the confusion and near chaos in industry and especially agriculture. In 1920 America opened its gates to 349,042 Italians, while 614,611 emigrated to other parts of the world, particularly South America. This was the last huge wave, because of subsequent severe restrictions on all immigration.

At first most of the immigrants naturally remained in New York, their point of entry. By 1880, they started scattering to other American cities. Farmers and fisherman were drawn far south and west, while manual workers were attracted by the promise of work to the mines of Pennsylvania and Virginia, the steel mills of Pittsburgh, the stockyards of Chicago and the factories and textile mills of New Jersey. According to Foerster's study, the 1910 census revealed the following regional distributions:

New England	13.2%		East South Central	0.7%
Middle Atlantic	58.6%		West South Central	3.0%
East N. Central	10.8%		Mountain	2.4%
West N. Central	2.6%		Pacific	6.0%
South Atlantic	2.6%			

And, as Foerster observed, it was a "strange result".[5] New York State had then about as many Italians as the whole country had

[4] Ibid

[5] Foerster, p. 328.

accommodated ten years before. If their children were added to this number the colony would have exceeded in population every Italian city except Naples. In no other city excepting New Orleans were they in first or second rank in 1910. In that year they numbered about 45,000 in Philadelphia and in Chicago, 31,000 in Boston and 20,000 in Newark. There were 115,446 Italians in New Jersey.

Little is known about the early beginnings of the Italian colony in Newark, one of the first and most important in the state. Legend intrudes on the few facts available. When Olindo Marzulli ventured into the early background and data of his countrymen to write "Gli Italiani D'Essex County", published in 1911, he explained in the preface "It is not easy to revamp a past which belongs to a generation of illiterates. Consequently, one is compelled to depend upon hearsay and original research.

Apparently before 1865 Italians were unknown in Newark, except for one Angelo Cattaneo, Gencese, who appeared in the Newark directory of 1865 as a "hatter" at 282 Mulberry Street. There is no evidence of a previous settler, although legend would have it that a person appropriately named "Garibaldi" was the founder of the colony. This mythical personage was supposed to have derived his name as a result of acquaintance with the Italian hero during his stay in America. The legend, which has no basis in fact, even held that "Garibaldi" served in the Civil War and died soon after a government pension had been awarded to him.

The United States Census of 1870 recorded 29 Italians in Newark and 257 throughout the State. Only seven, however. bearing names of

North Italian origin, were listed in the Newark directory of 1870-1.[6]
These have no descendants in today's colony, as far as is known. Two
of them were hatters, at 26 Orchard and 3 Garden Street (Cattaneo had
moved from Mulberry Street), and two were cabinet-makers who escaped
close competition by the distance between 136 Sheffield Street and
337 Warren Street. E.Z. Menchini's "Millinery" was at 155 Washington
Street. At 337 Market Street Luigi Gargiotta, harbinger of the host of
"Figaros" to come, conducted a barber shop. The seventh Italian,
Mary Alaboni, was a "widow" according to the laconic reference in the
directory. The scattered addresses of these Italians provide no
indication of the "quartieri" to follow.

The first large stream poured into Newark in the decade between
1870 and 1880. It had been preceded in 1869 by a group of Genoese who
settled on Bank Street. According to Marzulli they were G. Fernetti,
Giuseppe Dughi, Domenico Zanelli, J. Arardo and D. Grofatti, who were
naturalized in 1876. Stefano and Andrew Poli, brothers, together with
Carmine Mareglia and a few others built their homes in the then
picturesque Comes Alley. At about this time Alfonso Illaria and
Angelo Mattia set up combination taverns and boarding houses in anti-
cipation of the coming population boom. The first wave was an overflow from New York.

This decade's immigration was the first to be characterized by a
heavy preponderance of South Italians and Sicilians. These were simple,
rugged, quiet-living peasants and artisans from the agricultural

[6]Several Italians interviewed stated that they could distinguish North
Italian names from Southern but were vague as to how it was done.

province and hill towns south and east of Naples and from Sicily.
Bewildered by the garish, tumultous life of New York and its teaming
"little Italy", unhappy and uncomfortable in the sunless, cramped and
disease-ridden tenements of New York's slums, they set out to find homes
more suited to their temperament and background.

Newark, then a comparatively calm and spacious city, was the answer
to this nostalgic search of the thousands from the region of Campania,
Calabria and Sicily. Here, too, was the all-important lure of work, hard,
back-breaking work, for Newark was undergoing an industrial development
and population growth which required men, factories, miles of new tracks,
roads, streets, bridges, sewerage systems, schools and houses. These
combined advantages of labor demand and relatively pleasant environmental conditions drew Italians like a magnet. They came so thick and
fast that by 1880 the newcomers completely blotted out the handful of
Genoese who had preceded them. New Jersey was to their liking. As a
result, when wives, brothers, sisters and children were later sent for,
they were met at Battery Park and immediately whisked over on the ferry-
boats to New Jersey.[7]

The first Italian quarter in Newark was established in the neighborhood surrounding Boyden and Drift Streets. On Boyden Street they
encountered hostility from the Irish particularly, despite their common
religion. Fist fights and street brawls were common until the Italians
moved to Seventh and Eighth Avenues and the intervening streets and
alleys.

[7]For a typical account of the experiences of an Italian immigrant, see
Pascal D'Angelo, Son of Italy (New York: The MacMillan Co, 1924).

The topography of this section was an appropriate backdrop to the drama of the new Italian life in the staid Newark of that period. The "First Ward" colony still remains faithful to its prototypes famous from New York to San Francisco. Here, too, are mysterious, winding streets and alleys which earlier presented an even greater and more detailed fidelity to an Italian colonia.

Aqueduct Alley, evil and tortuous in its drop from Clifton Avenue to Eighth Avenue, even today represents an ideal stage-setting for a "dead end" drama of slum life. Its bleak tenements, now deserted except for a handful of Negro families, once swarmed with hundreds of families who imparted to it a rare flavor. The Italian housewives strung their clothes-lines from house to house, letting wash hang with charming informality over the alley. And it was not rare during the Prohibition era for the excess water from Monday's washing to mingle with the blood of local young blades who "lived dangerously" and met sudden death in the shadows of the close packed buildings. Such incidents, tending to give the area a certain melodramatic fame as a crime center, were incidental to the adaptation to American life and in no wise reflected the hard-working, honest-living majority.

The Italians here were and remain more gay and exuberant than their brothers scattered throughout various working-class sectors of the city. This spirit has found expression in numerous cafes, restaurants, pizzerie ovens, music stores, and open-air clam and oyster bars. In sound, smell and color the quarter is distinctly and proudly Italian. At night, particularly, life takes on a quickened and more colorful pace, reminiscent to the imaginative of Naples.

River Street, between Mulberry Street and the present McCarter Highway, was the center of the second Italian colony established in Newark in the decade 1870-1880. Now it is a busy thoroughfare lined with black, time-worn hovels occupied by a miscellany of vagrant families, fruit and banana houses and a mournfully long freight depot.

Only the sign CASAZZA & SON - Banana Importers - is a reminder of the days when this street was alive with hundreds of Italian families who had followed Michael Adubato when he opened his first lodging house on the block. The colony was not far from the river bank on which Newark's first English settlers, immigrants from Connecticut, landed in 1666.

The River Street colony flourished, and its overflow soon pushed east of the old Pennsylvania railroad station into the heart of the "Down Neck" section. By 1900 Italians, mainly from Nocera, San Gregorio, Buccia and Calabria, had moved along Ferry Street as far as Wilson Avenue (then Hamburg Place) and gradually filled all intersecting and parallel streets southward towards the port meadows and wasteland. The Italian occupation of the "Ironbound" era, displacing native American and previously established German groups, was symbolized by the sale of a Protestant church which around 1900 became the church of Our Lady of Mt. Carmel. It was on the corner of McWhorter and Ferry Streets, almost in the center of the slowly dissolving River Street and the rapidly growing Ironbound Italian quarter.

During the same period a new colony had its beginning in the Fourteenth Ward along Fourteenth Avenue and adjoining streets. The nucleus was mainly Sicilians, supplemented by families from the crowded First

Ward as well as by the constant arrivals from provinces south of Naples
who were attracted to all the Italian neighborhoods. By 1901 this Fourteenth Avenue colony which had started under the initiative of Antonio
Cerrato and Pasquale Villanova, its pioneer realtors, was large and
important enough to build its first St. Rocco's church on the corner of
Fourteenth Avenue and Hunterdon Street.

Thus in the period between 1870 and 1900 almost 10,000 Italians
made their homes in various parts of the city. These quarters still
house the basic Italian population of Newark, but their frontiers have
widened to embrace adjoining areas. This inevitable spread, due to a
variety of causes, was eminently desirable. It would not have been
otherwise with the gradual integration of the Italians with the greater
life of Newark, the rise in living standards of the Italian workers, the
public school education of their children and the belated but phenom-
enal growth of an Italian-American business and professional class.

CHAPTER III

EARLY LIFE IN NEWARK

Newark on the eve of the twentieth century offered an ideal center for Italian immigrants. Few other cities on the Atlantic seaboard, perhaps, were better suited to absorb an immigration overwhelmingly working class in composition and traditionally industrious. Enterprises new and old, which had played a vital role in production during the Civil War, had gradually transformed Newark from a modest, shopkeeping, small-scale production town into a thriving manufacturing and commercial center, looking forward to more and more expansion.

The Civil War had opened new vistas for the city and had carried it to a position of industrial importance. This development brought the city face to face with problems of expansion and improvement. In the fortuitous coincidence of growing Newark's industrial needs and the coming of the Italians is found the beginning of the occupational history of a group which was to play a conspicuous part in Newark's rise from a busy industrial city to a twentieth century metropolis.

Italian labor in Newark, examined historically, exemplifies the exploitation of a minority working class people by a vigorous, forward-moving industrialism careless of human values. It is a microcosm in which can be seen the genesis of Italian-American community life, a hegira of a bewildered people in search of an elusive American dream. It is a mirror reflecting the origin and nature of the prejudices and

discriminations which the early Italians suffered with the patience and
dignity of a people grown immune, though not resigned, to social
injustices.

Manual labor was the lot of Newark's first Italians. To them was
given the difficult, dangerous work of laying the structural basis of
Newark's industrial development. Railroads, transit companies and
municipal engineering departments were the first agencies to absorb
Italian labor en masse. Hired individually, in groups, or by contract
through the typical "padrone system", they worked by the hundreds in
sweating, griny gangs.

In the years following 1880 such groups of workers became a
familiar sight throughout the city and its environs. Endlessly, it
seemed, they swung picks and wielded shovels in the hot sun. Tirelessly
this huge army dug myriad ditches for gas and water and sewer lines,
spreading netlike over the expanding face of the city.

For the Pennsylvania, Central and Lackawanna Railroads and the
Public Service Corporation they constructed sidings, excavated rail beds,
laid miles of wooden ties and steel track. And upon completion of sewers,
streets and tracks the builders became the guardians of the fruits of
their toil. The Italian emerged as the sweeper of Newark's streets, the
cleaner of its sewers and the trackwalker of its railroads, in whose
hand the red flag added to the color of his bandanna-topped work clothes.

This was the price which Newark exacted as an entrance fee from its
early Italians who resignedly, sometimes joyfully, accepted menial tasks
abandoned by Irish and German workers who were stepping up the rungs of
labor's ladder, armed with the powers of a more rapid assimilation and,

in the case of the Irish, the open sesame of native speech. For many,
such jobs become a permanent method of earning their livelihood, for many
others, a temporary stop on the way to more suitable and less strenuous
activity, while quite a number contemptuously avoided such work, which
according to them was to be reserved only for unfortunate "Cafoni".[1]

The laborers not absorbed in construction work were swallowed by
factories, where, too, they were compelled to start at the bottom,
stepping into menial, unpleasant and underpaid jobs relinquished by native
or assimilated groups. Here, however, there was no mass labor demand
nor a convenient "Padrone" to arrange things for his countrymen. These
early Italians, of rural or artisan background, had no understanding of
modern labor techniques, problems or movements. When to this inexper-
ience was added their passionate desire to work at almost any wage so as
to send for their families, it can be understood how they incurred the
suspicion and hatred of Newark's laboring classes. Unscrupulous
employers sometimes found them convenient weapons with which to beat
down wages and hamper the nascent labor movement, then centered mainly
about the militant Knights of Labor. There are no records of actual
strike breaking by them. But a story in the New Brunswick Daily Home
News of August 8, 1887, regarding a widespread leather strike then
raging in Newark, relates that the Knights of Labor accused the leather
firm of P. Reilly & Sons of "employing a gang of Italians just to make
a show and give the impression that work is progressing in the shop."

[1] Peasants, with a connotation of uncouth or unlettered.

And according to the same paper, Mr. Reilly's rebuttal was that he "had not employed any Italians but put some Germans to work."

Despite such unfortunate misunderstandings and obstacles the Italians, quick to learn, rapidly adapted themselves not only to complicated machinery and new industrial techniques but also to American working standards. In a short time they were employed by the hundreds in the city's most important leather, jewelry, fur, cigar and metal factories and foundaries. The skilled tailors, hatters and dyers became desired and valuable assets in hat and clothing shops. This gradual but successful penetration, not only of local factories but also of those in surrounding communities, laid the basis for the eventual incorporation of these Italians into the general working class of the city.

Another important labor group -- artisans and building workers whose skill had been handed down from generation to generation -- quickly found outlets for their talents in the colony and in the community.

By 1911, when the first attempt of chronicling the colony's past was made by Olindo Marzulli, one of its leading intellectuals, the Italians were well on the way towards integration in the economic life of Newark. Following the "primordial period of its formation," as Marzulli expressed it, certain elements escaped from the wage-earner class. In the very brief essay on "Industry and Commerce" Marzulli comments, with an obvious mixture of pride and regret, that "our co-nationals no longer limit themselves to being barbers, boot-blacks or workers or farmers. Overcome by that spirit of enterprise which char-acterizes the American people they have entered almost all the branches of industry and commerce. The aspiration to a weekly wage sufficient to cover family expenses was extended to the point where it has become a need for expansion in the field of economic competition." And Marzulli, who then was somewhat socialistic, added that, "this need which reflects the conditions of capitalist society, has created even in our midst a class of business men."

Barbers, bankers, bakers, and bottle-makers were listed as the leaders of the growing class of entrepreneurs. With great confidence Marzulli wrote: "It can be said that the trade of barbering has been monopolized almost completely by Italians who have opened hundreds of elegant shops throughout the city." The bankers, though naturally less numerous, also were doing well, when it is considered that they had been grocers, laborers or tavern keepers. About them Marzulli wrote: "there is a flourishing loan and credit society, which has many clients among Americans. We have rich and solid banks like that of D'Auria." He neglected, somehow, to mention Vito Marzano's flourishing financial institution.

Starting as a clothing merchant in 1885 Marzano catered to the needs of his newly arrived countrymen. As was usual, his customers began to leave money with him for safekeeping until it was sent home.

By 1890, his business became almost entirely private banking. From then until 1925 when the bank was incorporated as the Marzano State Bank his primary service to his fellow countrymen was private banking. Later he changed the name to the Bank of Commerce.[2]

Bakeries, which at evening filled the colonies with the sweet fragrance of the bread of tomorrow, were "numerous". One owned by

[2]Italian Tribune, January 26, 1940.

Achille Basile employed 25 workers and "did business exclusively with Americans." Another firm employing Italian workers was the D'Amico Macaroni Company, which occupied large quarters on Drift Street.[3] The tailoring firm of Solimeni and Santoro employed almost one hundred of the colony's tailors at its sewing machines. Dominick Lo Prete owned "one of the best bottle factories." The predominantly German-Jewish jewelry industry of Newark had been successfully entered by the Messrs. Roberto, who owned "a first class jewelry shop employing fifty workers." F.R. Marsulli -- the historian hints at no relationship -- dealt in all liquids ranging from wines, anisette and vermouth to olive oil. The leading importers of the indispensable cheeses, oils, macaroni, tomatoes and salamies were listed as the Messrs. Cassese, San Geronimo, La Torracco and Montefusco. "Now," concluded Marsulli, "the colony is on the way of economic progress, which offers the hope that there will be the desired civil development and consequent increase in prestige." His hope and prophesy were realized with the passage of time.

Life, then, for most of these early Italians was hard, and each day brought its obligation of tiring labor on the side of a railroad track, at the excavated bottom of a street or in a sunless shop. Fortitude in the face of adversity and suffering, handed down from the century-long struggle against a degenerate Bourbonism, with which was merged the realism of an ancient peasant stock which counseled against expecting too much from life, rendered the difficulties of early adjustment tolerable.

One important factor in ameliorating the immigrants' lot were the social amenities attending marriages, births and deaths, which restored

[3]Now out of business due to a family quarrel.

the close communal and family associations of the old village life. The
first recorded Italian wedding in Newark was in 1877. It was that of
Arsenio Costa and the daughter of John Capuano, the colony's first under-
taker. The wedding was quite fittingly celebrated with exceptional
pomp and gaiety. Everybody was there. Peter Puglia, a '75 pioneer,
who had a farm on the corner of Clinton and Badger Avenues, and it was
he who supplied the homeland delicacies of broccoli and pot-cheese which
were spread lavishly on the tables. Alfonso Ilaria's tavern was emptied
to furnish the endless bottles of wine which inspired the guests to dance
to his sad massuccas and gay tarantella, in which he was accompanied on
the guitar by Alfonso Cervone, a baker.

This historic wedding set the pattern for a whole series which
followed quickly and at frequent intervals. Similar ritualistic
observances characterized the ceremonies attending baptisms and funerals.

Customs imported from the homeland showed peculiar new-world modifications. In the sunbaked villages of Southern Italy, birth, marriage
and death had taken place within a narrow frame of religion and tradition.
Christenings and weddings meant a brief period of gaiety marked by the
visit of close relatives and neighbors and the grateful receipt of a
handful of gifts in the form of food, clothing or live-stock.
Following a round of wine and a series of mutual salutations, work in
the field or shop was resumed. Funerals in the South Italian villages
were even more briefly observed. Embalming was unknown, and Italian
law forbade keeping a corpse in a house for more than 24 hours. So, at
sundown the simply shrouded, barefoot corpse, encased in a wooden box,[4]

---

[4]Sometimes enclosed in a casket which was rented over and over again for
the trip to the cemetery.

was carried or driven to the local cemetery, followed by a small cortege
consisting of the village priest, relatives, friends and sometimes
professional mourners. These ceremonies, stripped to the essentials,
called for little expense and were quickly dispatched to permit the mourners
to slip back into the daily round.

In an urban area such as Newark, where life was infinitely more
complicated and more directly under the supervision of municipal government, births, weddings and deaths took place amidst a welter of new
conditions. One all-important factor was expense, which had b en of
minor consideration in Italy. To leave the ha,hazard life of the "casa
a bordo"[5] and embark on marriage and home building, or to bury one's
dead, invariably involved more money than most had at their disposal.
This dilemma was solved by money contributions on the part of relatives,
neighbors, work mates and friends.

Couples contemplating marriage would extend verbal invitations to
the entire neighborhood. At the wedding feasts, held usually in a hall
or at the home of the bride's parents, guests in lieu of gifts presented
the bridal pair with white envelopes, called "buste", containing from
three to five dollars, or more, according to their degree of kinship or
prosperity. While the bride acknowledged the gifts with smiles, her
mother, seated beside her, tucked them into a black bag on her lap.
Sometimes the bride received the gifts in person. In exchange the guests
were entertained with guitar and mandolin music, dancing, copious wine
and sandwiches, especially prepared pastries and sweets, and, perhaps
most important, the unwritten promise that they would be repaid in kind

[5]Corruption. Literally, house to board.

if and when the occasion arose with them or their kin. Such contributions
played a considerable part in the calculations of prospective brides and
grooms. Ceremonies attending deaths and funerals were equally elaborate.
Here bodies were embalmed in accordance with municipal regulation and
thus could be kept in the house. Throughout America Italian undertakers
were instrumental in formulating the custom of "wakes", still preserved.

An Italian "wake" usually lasted three or four days. Palms, floral
wreaths and giant crucifixes hung over the coffin, which lay in the
principal room of the flat, preferably near an open window. Relatives,
neighbors, friends -- even mere curiosity seekers -- dropped in to
remain for a few minutes or many hours. Mourners were expected first to
express their formal condolences to the bereaved after which they proceeded to the rail at the foot of the coffin and offered prayer for the
dead. Then they would sit silently watching the dead or talking in
whispers in the dim candle-light.

Each guest was expected to enter the kitchen where on the table
stood a grey metal box beside a book. The mourner would put his contribution toward the funeral expenses in the "poste" box, listing his
address and the amount. This contribution assured a seat in the coach
if it was desired. People with cars would volunteer their services at
this time. Usually, a relative or friend of the deceased sat at the
table to watch over the "poste" and help those who could not write their
names. In the kitchen also the men gathered, garbed in rude work-clothes,
smoking gnarled pipes or stogies and drinking the wine which was
occasionally served. A safe distance from the lamentations of the women,
they discussed the eternal problems of life and death, or reminisced

about the departed and his numerous predecessors to the grave here or in
Italy. No cooking took place during a "wake", nor were meals served in
the house of the dead. The bereaved families were fed at the homes of
neighbors or relatives.

At midnight most of the mourners departed, but the body was never
left alone. Certain persons were asked to keep vigil in the kitchen
through the night, and volunteers could always be found. Three or four
men would be enough, joined later by others, and they spent the night in
the kitchen, repulsing the attacks of slumber by frequent sipping of
black coffee -- cafe espresso-doused generously with fragrant anisette.

The "poste" and "buste" then solved two specific and important
economic problems of people with no form of social security or mutual
benefit societies and who had not been in the country long enough to
accumulate savings. Such customs represented not only a valuable
material aid, but were an important factor in welding the young colony's
social life.

With the years, however, these formalities tended to degenerate,
sometimes into mere expensive displays exploited by morticians and
florists. "Poste" contributions often amounted to several hundred
dollars, particularly in the early days, upon the death of a person
known to many residents in the separate colonies. Normal funeral costs
were comparatively small, but out of respect toward the dead and under
the promptings of the undertakers, Italian families, for the sake of
social prestige, indulged in high-priced caskets, cars bedecked with
flowers, High Masses and tall monuments. Bands playing funeral airs
preceded the processions and with dragging steps and matched music,

the beloved lost one was escorted to the final resting place. This distortion of a practice rooted in a sense of generosity and solidarity has long been the wonder of native Americans, especially American undertakers.

As living standards of Italian workers improved, job opportunities increased, mutual-aid societies were established, and as industrial insurance was widely bought, the "poste", if not the "buste" custom, lost all real significance, although both remain to this day.[6] The prolonged depression, however, has frequently revived their original function.

The social life of Newark's early Italian, naturally, was not confined to observances of weddings and "wakes." Numerous other social activities intervened. The growing number of sacraments led to the establishment of four Italian churches between 1877 and 1901, and religion was soon playing an increasingly important role. This formalization of religion reflected the growing normalization of Italian existence. Hundreds of now forgotten or dimly remembered religious societies were established for men and women, centering their activities around the newly built churches.

Each South Italian town, village or province which had representatives in Newark organized a society in honor of its patron saint.

[6]Today the "poste" and "buste" survive mainly with the first generation, who give the white envelopes to the daughters of their contemporaries at weddings and in the old way at funerals. However, the second generation in return and among themselves have almost unanimously adopted the American gifts or flowers as the case may be. The more sophisticated and assimilated old people give the white envelope only to those whom they know to be part of the old pattern from previous marital or death occasions. Otherwise, they too send gifts or flowers. A large acquaintanceship means a considerable yearly expense to the very poor. Poverty must be extreme, however, to prevent the Italian family from observing the amenities of the situation.

San Gerardo, healer of the sick and crippled, and San Gennaro, defender
of Naples from the fiery wrath of Vesuvius, were the central figures of
cults which flourished particularly among Italians from the neighborhood
of Naples. Those from farther south, especially the Sicilians, those
of the Fourteenth Ward, held Saint Rocco and Saint Filippo Neri in
equal reverence.

It was these societies whose gay, carnivalesque feasts brought to
quiet, protestant Newark the riotous color and deep feeling of medieval
religious processions. The celebration of these "Feste" followed a
common pattern. The streets of the Italian quarters, particularly in
the First Ward, were gaily decorated under a panoply of brilliant
multicolored lights, banners and giant candles artistically arranged,
becoming veritable replicas of the old village feasts. Statues of the
revered Saints and Madonnas would be drawn along the streets, littered
with bunting, corn-cobs and empty clamshells, on the brawny shoulders
of sweating, happy and reverent workers dressed in their Sunday best,
their coats or shirts burdened with religious medals, badges and buttons,
and wreathed in red, green and white sashes with tinsel letters. They
would be followed by throngs of pious wives, mothers, children and
grandmothers, chanting prayers, often barefoot, dressed in somber
brown or black dresses of peasant simplicity, covered by dark or polka-
dotted aprons whose hems touched the cobble-stones. On their heads the
women wore the characteristic shawls to the amusement of native
Americans who lived to see their daughters revive this fashion in the
late thirties.

These annual celebrations took months of preparation, involving the formation of committees and arrangements with the churches. Many of these heads of committees emerged as the Italian political leaders. Individuals struggled for the prestige of being on leading committees and the societies vied to organize the most breath-taking spectacles. Usually they lasted from one to five days and were concluded with sensational pyrotechnic displays. To most native Newarkers such scenes were horrid examples of imported paganism and Popish superstition. Even Marzulli commented bitterly: "...in fact, they (the feasts) only serve one aim, that of having our people considered noisy, and lovers of outer display of faith, rather than faith itself." Critics did not seem to understand that such processions were an emotional outlet which helped make life in a strange country tolerable.

Early Newark Italians have left but a small heritage of secular institutions. Hundreds of mutual aid, "mutuo soccorso", societies, a few of which linger on, such as those formed by residents of Caposele, Calabritto, Basilicata, Buccino and Ariano di Puglia, were only lay reflections of similarly regional religious societies. Today only worn and tattered banners, lying in the chests of forgotten halls in the various Italian quarters, recall these pioneer organizations. They were succeeded by the better organized, financially sounder Sons of Italy (Figli D'Italia). But even this latter-day society, with all its resources, from the beginning fought a losing battle with insurance companies and that spirit of personal independence which American life had imparted even to the naturally cooperative Italians. Many of the mutual aid societies were gradually transformed into social clubs and became centers of miniature regionalism within a general circle of regionalism.

Another social activity was represented by efforts to commemorate important dates in Italian history, culminating in the legalisation of Columbus Day as a holiday in New Jersey. On the fourth centenary of his discovery of America, in 1892, the members of 32 Italian societies, under the leadership of G.M. Belfatto, Eugenio Corcia and Victor Bianchi, marched down Broad Street and placed a large bronze plaque of Columbus in the old City Hall. Following the first Columbus Day March, Marzulli wrote: "Other historic occasions were celebrated with greater or lesser solemnities."

On October 2, 1896, Dr. Negaro headed a committee which organised a parade on the occasion of the capture of Adowa in Ethiopia by Francesco Crispi's African Expeditionary Force; nearly fifty years later Italians responded to Benito Mussolini's successful campaign against Addis Ababa. In 1896 also Newark Italians celebrated the 26th anniversary of the capture of Rome in 1870 by the forces of unification.

But, according to Marzulli, "the truly grandiose celebration" was that held October 12, 1909. This was the first year in which the date of America's discovery was a legal state holiday. It must have been an impressive spectacle, for the usually critical Marzulli wrote: "...the parade seemed endless because of the hundred and ten societies which marched. This was the most powerful effort made by the Italian colony of Newark to show what splendid results could be achieved by organising for magnificent purpose." Since then Columbus Day Committees have been elected annually and appropriate ceremonies observed, particularly since the Giuseppe Verdi Society sponsored the erection of the Columbus Statue in Washington Park several years ago.

Other patriotic activities usually found the sponsorship of local lodges of the Sons of Italy, such as the celebration of the 50TH Anniversary of Italian unity when, says Marzulli; "The most intelligent and civilized element of the colony gathered, and demonstrated -- perhaps for the first time -- a seriousness of urpose which is vainly looked for elsewhere."

All these more or less forgotten processions, parades, and demonstrations, though today they might appear futile or anachronistic, served their purpose in their time. They were attempts of the early Italian colony to find itself, and in its search it happily and inevitably found something more -- the beginnings of participation and eventual integration with the life of Newark.

CHAPTER IV

ADJUSTMENT AND BEGINNINGS OF INTEGRATION

The primary adjustment which Italians had to make upon reaching Newark was that of language. Knowing only their own spoken dialect, they faced as difficult a problem as any immigrant group. Even had they wished to, many of them found that it was impossible for them to study English from books, as they could not read Italian. Lost in a strange world, they soon realized that the only system which offered any satisfactory group relationship was segregation. Each town in Italy had its counterpart on a street in some part of New Jersey. It was a transplantation without precedent in American history. A little group of people from a south Italian town would part in Italy and reassemble in Newark, Paterson, Trenton, Passaic, Jersey City or elsewhere. Their peculiar customs, and forms of social activity would also be transplanted, at least in so far as the American environment favored them.

Although social customs and language could make a relatively easy adjustment to American conditions by segregation, it was nearly impossible to transplant economic life. Coming from a peasant existence or small town shopkeeping, the southern Italian, particularly, became immediately a city worker or some kind of a railroad laborer. His vegetable garden was gone, his work was strange although unskilled, and the whole pattern of economic life was different. Crowded into tenements, the Italians found their only recreation and social existence in relationships with fellow townsmen. The more formal life of the city was bewildering in its coldness and formality. There were certain occupations, such as barbering and shoe repairing, which Americans left to the Italians, who thus obtained their only contacts with large numbers of people outside their own colonies.

In addition there were a multitude of American customs which it was hard to understand. Rent, for example, was never paid in produce. They had entered a strictly money economy. The food habits of the Americans were utterly strange. As a result Italian food stores sprang up to cater to old country tastes. Children, compelled to attend public schools and thrown together with those from other parts of Italy, began to make friends and later developed romantic interests. What was much worse to the older people, Italian boys a d girls became interested in those of other nationalities. Pressure from parents to stay Italian and pressure from the outside world to become a part of it led to conflicts between older and younger generations. This pressure was particularly difficult for the girls, who traditionally stayed at home in Italy or at least led a much more circumscribed existence.[1] There they were supposed to aid their mothers in some regions while in others they worked in the fields. At any rate there was little or no opportunity to meet members of the other sex as a rigorous segregation was practiced after the very early years. The Italian emphasis on virginity for the female led to strict control. Imbued with American

[1]See Chapter on Marriage.

ideas, girls resented the different treatment by their parents and their friends' parents. Inevitably parental control, so easy to maintain in Italy, lost its efficacy. Furthermore, commercial amusements tended further to disrupt the intense family formerly customary.

Clothing style, which had been standardised in Italy, became a factor in the thinking of the young people. Clothes became distasteful because of changes in style before they wore out. Hats, an affectation in the old country town, became a necessity here. To a lesser extent sons, too, demanded clothing which would make them less conspicuous among schoolmates.

The use of English intruded on the Italian dialect, and perforce the older people had to learn some of it. By its very complexity compared to the simpler Italian dialects, English produced a problem. The older people never did learn sufficient English to hold a conversation; while those in middle life, even if they had American contacts, retained a heavy accent. Even young people with some American schooling by no means spoke fluent English. The women of the colony had less need to understand American ways except as their children became a problem. Consequently their knowledge of English and their understanding of American life was considerably less than that of the men, who went out into the world to earn a living.

Even the church adjustment was difficult at first. There was a choice between joining the Irish or German Catholic Churches and starting little parishes of their own. Inasmuch as the ritual was not familiar, it was not long before Italian churches sprang up.

Prior to the south European immigration, the Germans and Irish were

the "foreigners". The latter particularly, because of their peasant
status in Ireland and lack of education, were at the bottom of the
social ladder. Various one hundred per cent organizations of the
character of the Know Nothing movement were started by American
Protestants. Thus there was already a considerable anti-Catholic feeling
before the Italians arrived. Their strange customs, speech, gestures
and dress, plus their more obvious physical differences, aroused a
superior attitude among natives. Even the Irish, forgetting the
prejudices they had encountered, in their turn were resentful of the
Italian invasion. Street fights were common between the two groups, and
violent mutual antipathy persisted for a considerable time.

The early arrivals headed directly for certain focal points,
usually saloons as clearing houses of necessary information. Here jobs
were secured either through the saloon keeper or a recommended padrone.
Workers banked their funds in these saloons until they had enough to
bring over wives, families and relatives. Living quarters were provided in a nearby boarding house, one of the most profitable and
ubiquitous businesses in the Italian sections. Frugal newlyweds would
settle in large hous s with the purpose of boarding a number of men.

Most of the first Italians to come to Newark were either raw youths
who either never had married or had to leave behind their wives, parents,
sisters and brothers. The "case a bordo", or boarding houses, usually
run by pioneer Italians in the city, were practical substitutes for the
family and social patterns left behind. They offered not only cheap
lodging and food but also played the role of mother, home and social
club. Here one met fellow-townsmen, learned where jobs might be found,

and mastered the first elements of Italian-Americanese. The men slept
and ate together, sometimes in the same bare room, and often worked
together on the same jobs provided by the same padrone. Back home it
was comforting to wives and mothers to know that they were under the care
of trusted "paesani" or "parenti."

Typical and earliest of these boarding houses was Angelo Mattia's
three-story place at 37 Boyden Street which he, a carpenter, had built
himself. Mattia, one of the first Italians in the city, was called
"Colombo" by friends. He, too, began as a ditch-digger, but after finding employment in the lumber yard of the wealthy John Struble, Angelo
started on the road of prosperity and prestige on which his compatriots
hoped to follow him. Mattia's hostelry worked on a curious principle,
a stranger to both the European and American plans. He extended two
weeks free board to newly arrived immigrants; so popular was his house
that they were expected to live elsewhere if they found jobs. They
were expected to leave at the end of two weeks even if unemployed.
Angelo's house had a large back yard with benches, tables and alleys.
Here after a grueling day's work they came to read letters from home,
play "briscola" or "bocce", or just sit around and let America and its
mysterious ways grow on them.

Another haven was Alfonso Ilaria's saloon, also on Boyden Street.
Ilaria, a master-musician, was referred to as the "King of Italy"
because his tavern was a center for authoritative news from the old
country.

The new arrival was interested in living as cheaply as possible
and saving money. At first the object was to return to Italy, where he

could buy a small business or a plot of land. Many, however, stayed and established themselves here; in that case they saved to bring over their families. For the unmarried youth the hope was ever present that he could return to Italy, and, as a prosperous American, select a dark-eyed beauty as his bride. The sketchiness and temporary nature of life "a bordo" were poor substitutes for the healthy, normal family life to which the immigrants were accustomed. Thus they were willing to work for low wages and under humiliating conditions that invited the hatred of natives and fostered the cupidity of employers.

As the men brought their wives, daughters and sisters over the family system of the Italians was soon modified. The return to normal family relationships caused a basis for a formal social pattern. In Newark and other cities of New Jersey the boarding house society still exists among more recent arrivals, the Spanish. Last in the series of refugees from European troubles, Spaniards today represent the stage of adaptation reached by the Italians thirty years ago, if allowance is made for the modern physical environment.

The gradual decline of the "bordo" system and the spread of normal family relationships naturally altered the social activities of the colony. They became more and more institutionalized and manifested themselves in the form of weddings, christenings, funerals and on a wider social scale in the form of religious feasts and procession, mutual aid societies and embryo political organizations.

In all these contacts lie the background of the feeling of Italians at present toward other national groups. Accustomed to a class society in Italy, the new arrivals tended to accept an inferior position in

America as natural. At the same time the new freedom aroused a sense
of resentment at the ridicule and contempt of the Germans, Irish and
other early boat catchers. On the other hand Americans were crystall-
izing their attitudes toward Italians and acquiescing tacitly in their
segregation.

CHAPTER V

THE FIRST WORLD WAR AND ITS EFFECTS

Of all the millions of New Americans received in the years past before the World War, the Italians formed a large part, if not the largest single group. The beginning of the war, however, immediately affected immigration. Countries which had been entirely willing to release their excess millions became acutely conscious of their value as soldiers. A shortage of shipping and blockade measures made the physical difficulties considerable. The wavering position of Italy throughout the first year of the war, with groups agitating for both sides, added a serious barrier.

In America the Italians followed the course of the war with great concern as to Italy's final role. The age-level of Italian immigrants in this country with its very high proportion of able bodied men brought many of them into the army when America entered the war in April, 1917. The present commander of the Italian American Legion Post in Newark estimated that between five and six thousand Italians from the city were in the fighting forces. In Trenton, of the total enlistment of 7,164 for the first four divisions, there were 601 Italians or about eight per cent. Of these some 16 lost their lives. It is estimated by Italian leaders that one of every five men in the army from New Jersey during the World War was Italian.

Just prior to the war, American industry had slackened and the resulting unemployment of course affected the unskilled Italian worker. During the war those who were not in the service had jobs at high pay. This period of service in the army and in vital industries probably hastened the integration of Italians into American life. It was an occasion where Italians were forced out of their segregated existence and compelled to participate in a common cause with other American groups. Just at a period when Italians were going through the transition to American ways of life, war intervened and created a tremendous movement emphasizing patriotism, "Americanism" and American ways of behaving. The wave of feeling in the country which for German-Americans made life exceedingly difficult also took a more general attitude that all things foreign should be suspect. The various one hundred per cent American movements of the war period and immediately after unquestionably hastened the assimilation process. This intense patriotism is easily discernible among Italians today, who will seriously state that they approve of both Mussolini's fascism and American democracy.[1] In explanation they say that different conditions in the two countries call for different political systems, or as an added point they will emphasize that Mussolini saved Italy from communism.

Another important factor is that during this period a number of Italians emerged as leaders because of their military or patriotic services. Even after the end of the war, concerted efforts were made largely through the schools and adult education programs to hasten Americanization.

The end of the war brought a new wave of migration, the final one before restrictions were clamped down. The dislocation of the American

[1] Written in 1940. Newer attitudes are discussed in later chapters.

economy, climaxed in 1921 and 1922 by a depression, resulted in pressure from all over the country for Americanisation and, as one of its effects, the stopping of immigration. A little bewildered at the anti-alien sentiment, Italians again retired to the segregated friendliness of their colonies, except that contact with the outside world had accelerated the desire of young Italians to Americanise for professional careers.

The golden age of the 1920's had its counterpart in prosperity for Italians, some of whom became employers, particularly in construction and garment working.[2] Furthermore, Italian colonies now had politically wise leaders who are willing to play the great game of local politics. Blocks of Italian votes became available and the sheer voting strength they represented made it necessary to take more and more Italians into political office. However, they were by no means proportionately represented.[3]

[2] See Chapter on work.
[3] See Chapter on political life.

CHAPTER VI

ITALIANS AT WORK[1]

Most of the growth of Newark's population during the expanding years up to the first World War was due to immigration, a large part of which was southern Italian. The Italian arrivals readily found work in new factories and on the railroads. Service trades grew to serve the new populace. The building trades had a remarkable expansion. Along with the housing growth went an extension of the city's services; city sewers and pipe lines required incessant pick swingers. Neapolitan airs and Sicilian folk songs mingled with the rhythm of the growing city and were sealed into its structure. The clothing industry started its flight from New York's high labor standards. Iron and steel plants welcomed thousands of workers.

To supply the specialized products dear to the Italians, early arrivals invested small savings in little neighborhood stores and prospered. Italian barbers increasingly displaced the Germans until finally they were serving the whole town. The fine art of the shoe builder in Italy became changed to shoe repairer, as the craftsmen could not compete with American mass production of shoes. Taverns, established

[1]The statements in this chapter about the present are dated in 1939 unless otherwise noted.

early in Newark, grew rapidly to serve the convivial drink of wine or beer after the day's toil.

Today Italians still dominate these occupations. However, there is a definite trend toward certain of them. It was found that one-seventh of those employed in Newark are still in unskilled occupations. Primarily they are laborers, who perform a multitude of back-breaking jobs on Newark's railroads and streets and in heavy industries. One quarter are skilled workers, primarily in the clothing industry and the building trades, where they have displaced the Jews and Irish respectively. In the second generation these proportions also hold, except that there are slightly fewer skilled workers. White collar work is only a small fraction of the total, engaging only one person in a hundred in the first generation, and even in the second only one in fifty. Sales work is also very limited among the Italian born. The children, however, show a proportion of 3 to 1 over their parents. *

A considerable number of the first generation own small stores, but only a third as many of the second generation do. The explanation is obvious. The stores are still in the hands of their founders, who are more familiar with the wants of their contemporaries, know Italian well and have no objection to long hours of work. In addition the second generation reflects a decreasing use of Italian products. Even when the old people die off there probably will be a less proportionate number of small stores among the second generation.

Professional people form a very small proportion of both generations, but the second generation has roughly twice as many as the first, and their number is increasing rapidly. **

*See Appendix IV
**See Appendix V

Fully three sevenths of the first generation and even more of the
second are unemployed. The second generation unemployment is due to a
number of causes: work habits were never as firmly established as in
the first generation; the prospect of long hours at hard work has never
been particularly inviting; and the depression has prevented the learning
of a trade for the past ten years as well as demoralizing the worker
and wrecking such skill as he had.*

In general, those interviewed were following occupations for which
they had originally trained. Considerably more were trained for white
collar and sales work in the second generation, however, than are at
present engaged in it.

Somewhat fewer than half of the first generation housewives
received training for business. These first generation girls in large
part were the children of men who had come over earlier and then sent
for their families. In Newark, the girls were sent to work to supplement the family income.[2] In Newark over one half of the first generation
immigrants came at the age of fifteen or younger, and these came as
children of immigrants rather than independently. The girls were sent
to work to supplement the family income and provide money for recreation
and American products. But the custom was less prevalent among those
born in Italy. Italian families have consistently tabooed sending their
girls into domestic service. Reasons for this attitude are based partly

[2]An excellent study of Italian women at work in New York City has been
published. Louise C. Odencrantz, Italian Women in Industry (New York:
Russell Sage Foundation, 1919).

*See Appendix VI

on fear for the morals of their daughters, and a conviction that domestic service is not a respectable occupation and fit only for inferior peoples. To a certain extent this prejudice has lessened in the suburbs and country due to the exigencies of the situation. Thus there are many domestic service positions available in the suburbs and more Italian girls are employed in this type of occupation. The employed men are mainly barbers, shoemakers, laborers and factory workers of various sorts.

Of 285 immigrant Italians born on the other side, 110 claimed that they have learned their present occupation in the old country. Even among American-born Italians, one in every twenty-one claimed to have secured occupational training in Italy. This estimate, however, is probably much too high.

There is a decided lack of Italians in the professions. There were no accounting firms, for example, until 1925, and at present there are only four. Architectural firms numbered ten in 1922 and reached 11 in 1925. At present there are again ten.

The practice of law, the doorway to politics, has had a consistent and steady increase. The number of Italian lawyers was 36 in 1922, 72 in 1930 and 112 in 1939. Their offices are concentrated in the downtown business area.

In dentistry there has been a steady rise. Starting with only two in 1922, the number has risen steadily until today there are 33 distributed throughout the town. One third of these are in the largest Italian ward in the city and an additional third are in the other two centers of Italian population.

Italian drug stores, again heavily concentrated in the Italian districts, rose from 28 in 1922 to a height of 40. This number remained steady from 1925 to 1935, but by 1939 the depression had closed up seven of them in the two largest Italian districts.

The number of Italians who have entered medicine has also been increasing steadily. Thus in 1922 there were only 33 doctors of Italian extraction. In 1939 this number had been increased to 107. Characteristically, they too are concentrated in the Italian wards, the largest number being in the first ward. It is noteworthy that there are only three or four Italian doctors in the fashionable high rent area downtown. On the other hand there is a decided tendency for the physicians to move to the better homes found on the suburban edge of the concentration of Italians.*

Italian professional men must consciously set to work up an Italian clientele. Thus to rise in occupational standing the Italian is forced to be an Italian lawyer, druggist, doctor or dentist.*

Inevitably the young Italian who has completed his training and is ready to enter his profession is given a sendoff by the colony. A committee is formed from among friends of the family to organize a banquet in honor of the young hopeful. Care is taken to have as speakers at least one old friend of the family, one prominent, well-established member of the same profession, and one prominent non-Italian, preferably a politician, who is considered friendly to the Italian population. The local Italian press publicizes the event, the qualifications and personality of the young man are thoroughly discussed by the colony and another career is launched.

*The professional men were classified as Italian by picking Italian names from telephone directories. This may seem an unreliable method, but Italian names are easy to distinguish and the incidence of Americanized names has not been significant. This method does not distinguish people of mixed nationalisty and is deficient in this respect.

The Italian population is large enough to support a professional class within itself. These men live within a circle of acquaintances, clients, customers and patients which is neither Italian nor American but partakes of both and emerges with a brand new identity. It is only the exceptional man who manages by sheer ability to widen the orbit of his service. Among older immigrants such as the Irish and Germans this phenomenon has been broken down.

The general attitudes of Italians toward working in America and the prejudices which they believe to exist were investigated in Newark.*
Almost one half of the Italian born are cognizant of job discrimination based on their nationality because they are Italian, and of these almost one quarter are strongly aware of it. Only one quarter disclaim the idea that being Italian hurts their job opportunities, the remainder do not know whether it is a factor or not. A similar response is received from second generation people, except that fewer did not know whether there were discriminations or not, and more denied that there was discrimination of any kind. The relatively greater acceptance of the second generation by Americans is here revealed.

The Italians in New Jersey have been particularly hard hit by the depression due largely to prejudices against them and lack of training, which makes them subject to layoff in industry. It may be seen from the start that although the Italian foreign born constituted only 22 per cent of the foreign born population in the state in 1930, they numbered 42 per cent of the relief clients in 1937. In Essex County, although only 24 per cent of the foreign born are Italians, 50 percent of the foreign born relief clients are of this nationality. Generally,

*Data from the general questionnaire.

them, the urban Italians have twice as many on relief as their proportion in the population. One other item is interesting in connection
with the Italian relief population. On the other hand they show only
a quarter of their numbers as unemployables, as contrasted with the
Germans who show about one half unemployable. This is due to the earlier
German immigration. Many German immigrants have now reached the higher
age categories.

One other job source is open to the Italians. Unsuccessful as they
have been in securing elective jobs, they do much better in appointive
and civil service positions. Out of a total of 6,240 jobs in the
city departments, 1,046 or over 16 per cent are Italian. A complete
nationality breakdown of the city departments is given below.

MUNICIPAL EMPLOYE S[2]

DEPARTMENT	TOT.	ITAL.	JEWS	GER.	POLISH	IRISH	OTHER
Public Affairs	1730	516	151	208	16	252	587
Revenue & Finance	280	64	37	46	5	121	7
Public Safety	2006	73	109	612	42	1075	95
Public Works	1924	346	368	289	52	753	116
Parks & Public Property	300	47	27	28	5	177	16
GRAND TOTAL	6240	1046	692	1183	120	2378	821

In 1939 a total of 161 Italian industrial manufacturers were

[2]Figures compiled from names on payrolls of city departments.

tabulated in the city of Newark, employing 4,073 workers. Of these firms
there were 68 clothing firms who employed 3,278 employees.[3] Almost without
exception these businesses are not heavily capitalized.

An Italian cutter or presser in boom times could easily break away
from his employer and open a small shop of his own, with little capital.
Next to the service trades this constitutes the largest Italian occupational field. This analysis gives some idea of the extent to which the
garment industry has been Italianized.

STORES

The little Italian stores of various types lend considerable color
and an old world flavor to the Italian colonies. Familiar items are
displayed, and their use lends to the Italian immigrant a sense of
familiarity with his surroundings. Bakeries and groceries are the most
prominent of these stores. Ordinarily the bakery makes only bread of
many varieties, named usually after the shape and size of the ingredients.
One Italian baker product, pizza or Italian ie, has achieved considerable fame in the general community. It consists of a very thin crust,
open and filled with alici (anchovies), mozzarella (cheese) or pomidoro
(tomatoes). They vary from the normal pie size to huge rectangles or
circles. These bakeries have large delivery services. Pastry shops
operate independently of the bakeries and make a large variety of
Italian and sometimes French pastries. Usually they run rather high in
price. Most Italians dislike American bread, considering it too doughy.

[3] Manufacturers Industrial Directory of New Jersey, 1939. Bureau of
Statistics and Records, New Jersey State Department of Labor.

Many brought their own dough to the baker and a few still do.

The groceries with their redolent cheeses, garlic, salami, and red pepper hanging from the rafters and their cases of various brands of macaroni give promise of gustatory delights, as the nose realises that here are unusual foods. There are over 150 different types of macaroni, the general term, of which spaghetti is one. Olive oil, imported and domestic, in all price ranges, is a staple, as it is used in most Italian cooking. All kinds of olives and cheeses have big demand. Green coffee beans are sold for roasting at home.

The stationery stores, fewer in number, have many items which are uniquely Italian. Almost all of the merchandise is imported from Italy, and sells at moderate prices. Anything from a postal card to a complete set of Dante's works may be bought. The best selling items are the Italian publications: newspapers, magazines, books, love story serials, bibles, current events, booklets and music orchestrations.

THE COOPERATIVE FAMILY ASSOCIATION INC.

Twenty Italians from the Region of Veneto established the Cooperative Family Association, the first attempt to bring to Newark the benefits of cooperatives then widespread in Northern Italy. This together with similar associations in Hoboken, Clifton and Union City purchase food products collectively. The primary purposes of the association have been to form a colony and culture center for Venetians in North Newark and to achieve savings through collective buying.

In 1922 each of the 20 founders invested $30 for incorporation and decided that no one could purchase more than one share of stock. Their first store opened in May 1922 and 155 Verona Avenue. One half of the store sold imported and domestic groceries and dairy products, the other half, meats. At the end of the first year the membership had increased to more than 200, and this doubled within the next two years. In addition, non-members of other nationalities patronized the store.

In June 1924 the group purchased a three-story building at 853 Summer Avenue in North Newark. This contains a store in front and a large dance and recreation hall in the rear. They later bought properties adjacent to 853 Summer Avenue, where they built a modern live chicken market and then a tavern. The depression has somewhat retarded the growth of the organization, but it is still profitable. It organizes picnics in the summer and social affairs in the winter. At all these functions Venetian customs and traditions are observed.

The membership of the Association demands that its administrators be all men, well grounded in cooperative principles and dedicated to their principles. The officers of the board, a president, a vice president and a secretary are elected at an annual meeting.

TRADE UNIONS

In Newark at present the best organized trades among the Italians are the needle trades, represented principally by the I.L.G.W.U., the Amalgamated Clothing Workers and the Fur and Leather Workers. In the service trades the Italians are well organized. Many Italians have risen to prominence on the wave of union organizing fostered by the NIRA and NLRA. Italian opinion in Newark seems to be that the union

movement is doing a fairly good job of creating tolerance among racial
and national groups. Locals, however, still tend to be organized on
national lines, as the most convenient basis.

Estimates of Italian trade union strength run between 5,000 and
8,000 men and women. Women workers have been particularly hard to
organize, particularly young girls, who frequently encounter parental
disapproval of trade union activities. Although the Italians were late
in starting they are today prominent in the labor movement.

Since unions were known principally in North Italy, the south
Italian and Sicilian immigrants proved difficult prospects for American
organizers. In addition to lack of trade union experience, wage conditions in Italy were so bad that even a non-union shop in America
represented an improvement. Moreover, those who had come to America
through the efforts of a relative were conscious of loyalty to these
men for their passage money.

According to Joseph Cozzolino, now deputy to the Newark Commissioner
of Revenue and Finance, the first group of Italian workers to become
unionized were the stone cutters, about 1910. Soon afterward laborers
on construction work, bricklayers, carpenters and plumbers were organized in the great drive of the American Federation of Labor.

The leather factories and tanneries of Newark, constituting one of
the oldest industries in the state, have employed a succession of
immigrants. At first these were largely Germans and Irish but the
south Europeans, principally Greeks and Italians along with Poles,
have replaced them. There were many spontaneous strikes and demands
from the leather workers, but no union had much of a foothold until

the National Leather Workers Union came on the scene in 1934. The union
was joined with the fur workers and is now called the International Fur
& Leather Workers Union, C.I.O.

Thomas Gallanos, young Greek-American business agent of Local 27,
who has been one of the leaders of the Union since its inception, credits
the growth of it to the militancy of both the Italian and Greek workers.
At present Local 27 has 720 members, 35 per cent being of Italian origin,
about equally divided between first and second generation. There was
a time, before the Union was organized, when Italians formed more than
50 per cent of the workers in the industry. Their number has gradually
decreased.

A majority of the Italians in the local had never been affiliated
with any union until the Leather Union began its campaign. It was no
simple task to organize among this group. Besides promoting the
principles of trade unionism in front of the factory gates, the organizers
had to visit Italian colonies, canvass from house to house, and dis-
tribute circulars and newspapers in the native language of the workers.
The intensive campaign resulted in organizational victories in a
number of the largest leather factories.

For a number of years the union published educational material in
Italian. This practice was stopped in 1938, since it was felt that the
Italian worker no longer had difficulty in reading English.

Local 140, International Fur and Leather Workers Union, has 900
members, all employed in one of the largest fur factories in Newark.
Many other shops are organized, but all are much smaller and employ only
from 5 to 25 workers.

The fur industry has had many acute strike struggles, which on a
number of occasions resulted in blood-spilling. James Leonardi,
business agent of Local 140, claims that racketeers assured employers of
protection to valuable furs and at the same time violently combatted the
unions. These struggles were limited mostly to New York City, the
largest fur market in the world. It was inevitable, however, that they
should affect the industry throughout the metropolitan area.

The union claims that for a period of years employers were able to
create bitter feelings between Jewish and Italian workers. Through the
introduction of piece work they made the Jew and Italian blame each other
for the subsequent speed-up and lower wages.

The Jewish workers were the first to respond to the call of the
union. When a breakdown of negotiations between the company and
employees forced a strike, many Italian workers hesitated in going out,
and the strike was lost.

By exerting such pressure on the Italian workers the company felt
secure from any union progress.

Company officials, seeing the growing sympathy of their workers
for the union, organized a company union of their own. "Beer and sandwiches were generously given to the workers at meetings," says
Mr. Leonardi, "but nothing was ever done in bettering conditions the
workers petitioned for."

Organizers continued canvassing and issuing circulars and newspapers
in Italian. Slowly the workers joined, one by one, until a majority
belonged to the union, which today is firmly established.

For one and a half years the union printed special Italian bulletins.

This was stopped in 1938, the leadership feeling that the Italian workers were no longer backward in trade union principles and that better progress could be made by encouraging them to study English. On various occasions the Italian workers attend special meetings to hear speakers on the labor movement.

Of the 500 members in Local 140 of Italian origin, one third are first generation Italians. Six members of the executive board of 15 are Italians.

As early as 1900 clothing shops, encouraged by billboards, newspaper ads and chambers of commerce, were moving here to escape the unions in New York. The flow of Italian immigrants offered a cheap labor market which was difficult to organize. The clothing industry was the first field, other than heavy laboring, in which the Italians were employed in large numbers. At this time industrial homework was prevalent, hours were long, and wages were low.

The International Ladies Garment Workers Union undertook to organize the clothing workers. Its agents faced the hostility of employers and police and sometimes of ministers, and all in all had one of the most difficult problems in the history of trade unionism. Mr. Crivello, Manager of Local 144 of the I.L.G.W.U. in Newark, relates the following experience. "In 1918, one of the judges made it very clear to me how unwelcome the union was. I tried to explain that the shop being picketed was a runaway shop from the union which had come to New Jersey to pay starvation wages to the workers. The judge interrupted shrilly: 'The law is not concerned with that. These workers are free workers and they don't want to belong to the union. Hoboken is a peaceful town and we don't want any trouble. Stay away, young man, from these shores or you'll land in jail....your fine is $10 this time and it is cheap'."

Organizers speaking the language of the foreign workers operated in all sections where the particular national groups lived and worked. The first response came from the Jewish skirt and cloakmakers, who formed Local 21 of the I.L.G.W.U. in Newark in 1919. Historical data referring to the growth of Local 21 is written in Yiddish. In the last few years the Italians have displaced the Jewish workers in this phase of needle trade work and today are an overwhelming majority in Local 21.

The organization of Local 21 stimulated efforts in other branches of the industry. In 1921 a report describing the working conditions among the New Jersey waist and dressmakers was submitted to the international union, which thereupon intensified its work.

The foreign born workers had been taught to see only the suspicious evil in the union representative. It was not rare for the organizer to be chased down the stairs of a worker's home by some irate relative. Only after constant efforts were the union agents permitted to enter the homes of the workers and to speak to them. The answers they usually received in discussing the union were: "I would like to join the union, but I am afraid to be found out and then -- good-bye job! And how will we be able to live without a few dollars that I make in this shop, now that nobody else works in my family?" And the relatives of the worker would join the chorus: "Father is too old and Toto was injured on the job. We owe for three months rent. The baby is sick and we haven't any money for the doctor." So touching were these tales and scenes that the hard-boiled organizer sometimes left a few dollars on the table to buy food for the family.

Often, before committing himself, the Italian worker wanted to consult his priest. On occasions the union agent was invited to visit the priest. "If Father Lorenzo has no objection, we'll come to register our names with the union." "Such negotiations were rarely successful," stated Mr. Crivello.

It was a never-ending, difficult task. "Approaching the workers in the morning a few blocks away from the shop"...."Seeing them run in alarm to the factory, screaming for the police"...."Following them in the evening to find out where they lived"...."Trying to speak to them in their homes"...."Going to meetings of their Societies 'di Mutuo Soccorso and Loggie dell 'Ordine dell' Figli D'Italia, to which their husbands, brothers, fathers belonged." "The union appealed to their humanitarian feelings, their civic sense of dignity, their religious sentiment and patriotic pride," added Mr. Crivello.

Insurmountable obstacles were met when a _paesano_ or _paesana_ or _compare_ happened to be foreman or forelady in the shop. "Oh no, I cannot do that to the _Padrino_ (godfather) of my dear Gigi!"...."I won't repay with disloyalty to Don Saverio, my paesano, who put in a good word for me with the _Banchista_, who sold me, on credit, the ship ticket for my wife when I called her to come to America.

Newark, in 1922, saw the first general strike in the dress industry. An office was set up in the Workmen's Circle Lyceum, 190 Belmont Avenue, a large meeting hall was rented and soup kitchen arrangements completed. On August 16 the general strike was declared.

On August 25 an agreement was signed between the union and dress contractors granting the union recognition, 35 hours a week and minimum wages representing as high as 200 per cent increases. Press operators, who represent the majority in the trade, were guaranteed minimums of $22.05 and $28.35 weekly, depending on their line of work.

A month later these new members were chartered as Local 144, with over 2,000 members. Anne Sosnovsky, an active unionist trained in Local 25, was installed as manager, an office she held until 1934 when ill health necessitated her resignation and Antonio Crivello replaced her as manager.

In 1926 the International Union was torn with internal factional troubles and strife. Open shop employers eagerly seized this opportunity to try to further their own ends. To meet this menace differences were settled by individual leaders and they joined forces to reestablish the union.

Antonio Crivello is regarded as the leader of Italian trade unionists in Newark. Since 1904, when he became a skirtmaker, he has dedicated his services to the garment workers. On various occasions he was assigned to work with some of the shops in Newark but did not take up permanent residence until his appointment as manager of Local 144 in 1934.

Mr. Crivello was born in Palermo, Italy, in 1888. His mother wanted him to prepare for priesthood, and at the age of 11 he was admitted to the Cathedral of Palermo. From his early childhood he attended labor meetings with his father, who belonged to the Workers Fasci and was a follower of Nicola Barbato, the Sicilian socialist leader. He was expelled from Palermo's Catholic Seminary for propagating socialistic ideas.

Persecuted for political ideas, his family was compelled to migrate
to America in November 1903. Crivello immediately became involved in the
American labor movement and was especially active among the barbers and
the ladies' hat makers (whom he helped to organize). He married in
New York in 1912 and is the father of four children, all of whom are in
some way affiliated with trade union movements.

He first became an officer of the I.L.G.W.U. in 1917 and was
secretary-treasurer of the New York Joint Board between 1930 and 1933.
Following the epic-making dressmaker's strike in 1933 the union
succeeded in organizing the entire dress industry, swelling the membership of the Dressmakers Union in the Metropolitan area from 7,000 to
more than 120,000.

Once, when attacked by some individuals who wished him removed,
Mr. Crivello wrote: "Although an Italian by birth, I am an inter-
nationalist. As such I consider the children of all nations my sisters
and brothers. I am a person that preaches tolerance and respect for all
nationalities. At the same time, I condemn all wrongs whether done by
Italians or by any other nationality and whenever I can, I help in order
to rectify them.

"When I was sent to Newark, I came to fight two Italians who were
creating troubles to our organization with the intention of capturing
its administration. Due to my declarations regarding my internationalism,
I was misunderstood by a number of persons, but those who saw the light
understood that I was for liberty and justice....

"When workers insulted the Jewish race, I insisted that they be

punished and condemned by the union. I felt very much aggrieved and out-
raged when an injustice is committed against any nation, whether Jewish,
Spanish, Chinese or otherwise. This is publicly well known, not only
through my speeches but also through my writings....

"But while I preach respect for the other nationalities, I preach
also respect for the Italians. The Italians pay respect and demand
respect.

"Still living in our minds is the memory of the scenes of abuses,
outrages, persecution and exploitation to which the Italians were sub-
jected at the hands of unscrupulous employers before the Italians
organized themselves. It is fresh in our memory that most important
reason why the Italians fought....for the creation of Italian locals.
That reason was: RESPECT! RESPECT! RESPECT! And while in those days
the insinuations against the Italians were that they were unable to
administer their things, now it is generally recognized,.....that the
Italian locals are equal, if not superior, to the other locals."

Mr. Crivello, who from his early youth has been interested in
writing poetry, is known as a writer in Sicilian dialect as well as in
formal Italian and English, though his poetic ability has won him wider
recognition.

Since 1934, when Mr. Crivello took over Local 144, the union has
consistently strengthened and consolidated itself by being alert to the
economic, social and educational needs of the membership. Classes are
conducted in labor problems, current events, history of the union,
Parliamentary procedure, citizenship aid, dramatics, Italian and choral
work. The slogan in all material issued by the union is: "Join Your

Classes and Get A-Head!" Over 1,000 members have participated in the classes, which have an attendance of 25 to 60. At the end of each educational season diplomas are presented to the best students, who then are permitted to participate in the contest, with a prize of three week-end vacations in the Pocono Mountains.

Meetings are held monthly (suspended during summer months) at which reports of union activity are given and special speakers address the membership. Socials, dances and parties are a regular feature of the union's recreational life. All these affairs are enlivened by "local talent".

Two thirds of the members are Italian, and the remainder are Negroes, Jews, Polish, Germans and Hungarians. All these groups work harmoniously in maintaining and strengthening their organization.

Since 1938 Local 144 has published a monthly bulletin, "The Voice", with articles and news from the members, in English and Italian. The introduction to the first issue states: "We want this bulletin to be the voice of our members, American, Italian, Jewish, Spanish, Polish, German, Negro, all the different races and nationalities, who are equal in the union and face the same enemies and share the same problems."

Local 24, Amalgamated Clothing Workers, has had a membership fluctuating between two and four thousand in the past six years. Officials claim that out of the present total membership of 2,500, 95 per cent are of Italian origin. Of these 35 per cent are Italian women, half of whom are in the first generation group. Of the 60 per cent of males 35 per cent are first generation Italians. Almost all of the members lost in the membership fluctuation were first generation Italians.

Because of the frequent slack seasons in the clothing industry many workers sought jobs in other fields and remained at them. Contractors, who are the majority of employers in Newark's clothing field, have contributed to the drop by removing their shops.

The women take in homework, specializing in folding and collar preparing. They were brought into the union under the NRA in 1934.

The men are more active and take a greater interest in the union. According to Mr. Naiman, secretary-treasurer, Local 24 has not been as successful in developing women leadership as have other sections of the country. No social or educational activity is carried on by the union at present. The educational work that is done is encouraged by the General Office in New York through correspondence courses. Of the 27 members on the local executive board 24 are Italians, two Jewish and one Pole.

Almost all the employers are Italians, former workers in the industry, in which the employers at first were all Jewish. The Jews sold out to the Italians or went bankrupt, leaving room for skilled workmen to gather up the small jobs offered by the New York manufacturers, still predominantly Jewish. There are no manufacturers of any importance in Newark. The contractors specialize in making coats, vests or pants. They are organized into a Contractors Association and have set up a special fund to assist those in difficulties. Their main job has been to maintain standard prices, to share work equally and to prevent cutthroat competition.

Italians form the majority of the 254 members in Local 195, Journeymen and Tailors Union, an affiliate of the Amalgamated Clothing

Workers, C.I.O. The union had no special difficulty in organizing the Italian workers. In describing former working conditions Gerard Chiari, business manager of the local, said that the men received $16 a week and worked as much as 84 hours. The union has been able to win a 40-hour week with a $30 minimum wage and a one-week vacation with pay.

With one or two exceptions the Italians in the union are of the first generation. The remainder includes Greeks, Portugese, Poles and Jews. Of 13 members on the executive board, 10 are Italian, two Jewish and one Ukrainian. According to Mr. Chiari all of the employers in the tailoring industry who deal with the union are Jewish.

In general the Italians entered the industry in this country as skilled tailors having served their apprenticeship in Italy.

No specific educational or social activities are conducted by the union.

Mr. Chiari had been a tailor all his life before becoming business manager. He was born in Naples in 1896.

Of 2,200 members in the District Council of the Carpenters Union only 200 are Italians, and the majority of them are members of one local.

John J. Walsack, secretary-treasurer of the Carpenters District Council had very little information to give regarding the Italians in his union. Those Italians that are carpenters today, he said, learned their trade in Italy and were skilled workmen when they came to America.

The Italians have always been a small minority in the union. In 1885, when the Carpenters Union came into the A.F. of L. from the Knights of Labor, many Italians were active in the work of the union. No detailed material on the approximate number of Italians, or the

Italian leadership of the union, could be obtained.

Because of the great decrease in construction during the last decade, the Bricklayers and Plasterers Union in Newark has declined from 2,000 dues-paying members in 1929 to 700 today.

Of the 1,300 members lost 300 were Italians, many of whom were of the first generation. Of the present membership 200 are Italians, about evenly distributed between first and second generation.

The union had no difficulties in organizing the Italians, the majority of them had served the necessary four-year apprenticeship in Italy and had joined unions there before the rise of fascism.

One of the first places they visited on coming to this country was the union hall, where their Italian union cards were accepted as valid. The union has never organized any special activity around the Italians.

The State Journeymen Barbers Union was organized in 1910 by a number of locals from all over the state. At present the union has 8,000 dues-paying members. It has sought legislation to standardize the business and succeeded in obtaining municipal ordinances limiting the number of hours and a state sanitation law that to some extent limits the number of shops. Although some states have legislated to control prices, New Jersey has not done so to date, and during the depression the industry has faced the problem of price cutting.

Local 222 in Newark has about 400 members, of whom 85 per cent are Italians. About half the barbers in the city are not organized.

CHAPTER VII

ITALIAN FAMILY LIFE IN NEWARK

The family life of Newark Italians, though essentially a contin-
uation of the form which prevailed in Italy, has undergone modifications through a generation of adjustment to life in a major American
industrial city. These modifications are the result of conflict,
frequently painful, between the first generation, which clings to the
old traditions and the second which tends to respond to the impact of a
new environment. The modification is still in process with the emergent
interests of the third generation looming on the horizon.

Family life in Italy, especially in the Southern provinces, held
the highest place in the scale of Italian values. The word family
covered a wide field of relations which included grandparents, aunts,
uncles and sometimes godparents. Family life was considered the noblest
essence of existence, the purpose and end of the earthly life of man and
woman, and thereby exalted in popular thought, religion and art. In
these parts of Italy the family was not only the primary social unit but
the main agency for transmitting culture.

Two major influences had exerted a profound effect on the form and
content of family life in South Italy. The first and most important
was the Roman concept of paterfamilias, which in practice meant the
absolute control of the father over his family and in its affairs; the

other was the Christian principle of woman's role in life as wife and mother, the bringer of religious grade and ritual to the home, its vessel of tenderness. A wife was also the humble and obedient servant of her husband, the careful guide of his home and his children.

Within the South Italian family groups themselves there reigned an elaborate and carefully graded set of privileges, duties and mutual relations of respect. Children were taught from early age to respect the judgments and wishes of the parents, particularly the father, above all else. In South Italy children addressed their parents, as well as strangers and elders, with the formal, polite "you". However, in the North, the familiar "thou" was used among all members of the family. The eldest son had certain perogatives not enjoyed by his usually numerous brothers and sisters, he often superceded the mother as the father's confident. He was expected to assume family leadership upon his father's death. The eldest son was allowed to bring his bride to his father's house to live.

The South Italian family made a veritable cult of the mother. Although husbands made few outward or public expressions of affection, their attitude toward and treatment of wives was characterized by deep love and respect. The mother managed the economic life of the household, keeping all wages brought in by the husband and children. She was expected to be an example to the children in strict obedience to the head of the family. On his part the husband had to furnish to the best of his ability the wherewithal to keep the house going, so that the family be not disgraced by poverty. The opularity and prevalence of folksong sentiment, often touched with real pathos, glorifying mothers

dead and alive, such as "Sense Mamma", "Mamma Mia Nu Cnianna Chiu" and
"Una Cartolina a mma"[1] attest to the affection and esteem in which
motherhood was held in South Italy. South Italians, even the children,
frequently made oaths to the dead memory or living honor of their mothers.
Many Americans are familiar with the popular Italian exclamation "Mamma
Mia!"

The relations of the children to their parents were rooted in respect
and duty not only towards the father and mother but also to the traditional moral and religious codes handed down from one generation to
another. Until about the fourth or fifth year children of both sexes
were allowed to play together, even in quasi-nudity because of the
climate or the lack of clothing. But after these ages male and female
children were rigorously segregated in work, school and play. But play-
time was not for long in the South Italy of the 70's and 80's. After a
year or two of haphazard schooling, if they received any at all, the
boys were sent to the fields or apprenticed to an artisan in the village.
Education for girls was considered irrelevant and immaterial to their
future function as wives and mothers. Sometimes they were sent for
short periods to church schools to learn embroidery, but usually
following the seventh or eighth year their mothers kept them at home to
weave or knit and learn general domestic routines.

Girls and young women were kept under a more rigorous routine than
their brothers. A girl's good reputation and chaste demeanor were
considered of the highest importance. As in any provincial community,

[1]Neapolitan dialect.

Italian families were hemmed in by the taboos, restrictions and vigilance of their neighbors, many of whom were relatives and friends. Brothers considered themselves the protectors of their sisters and the family honor; in general their relations with girls of the village were predicated on this chivalrous concept.

Male children, although enjoying comparatively greater freedom than females, rarely deviated from the behavior framework set down by the parents. So great was the filial respect for the father, particularly in Sicily, that when father and son were seen talking together it was sometimes hard to accept the fact that a blood relationship existed between them.

Early marriages were the universal rule in these villages. Girls were considered ripe for marriage at the age of 15 or 16. It was, perhaps, the prospect of this early release from parental restriction that led the young girl to accept the code with patience. There were few cases of "romance" in the American Hollywood manner. Marriages were arranged, or at least suggested, by parents or relatives. If two young people took their own initiative in this respect it was usually done through a third party, as aunt, uncle, godparent or the general village busy-body, whose talents ranged from warding off the evil eye to match-making on a commission basis. The third party would bring the "masciata",[2] literally "the message", to the parents of the person desired. If the "masciata" found an echo, a marriage was arranged. There was no period

---

[2]Dialect. Other terms are Imbasciata or ambassador, which is good Italian. Sometimes a female arranger was called ruffiana.

of engagement, only a snort phase of courtship restricted to a few well-supervised meetings between the two young people.

Dowries, consisting usually of 20 sheets of linen and perhaps a family heirloom, went with the bride. The groom generally received a monetary gift from his parents, usually representing savings from his own earnings through the years, or the result of a hurried trip to the village usurer or some more affluent person. Honeymoons were rare; usually a bridal couple went off for a few days to the house of a relative in a nearby village, after which they returned to settle with or near their parents.

Few scandals marked the quiet life of these villages. Once a couple were "sistemate", settled, life forged ahead down preestablished roads. Divorce, separation and illegitimacy were so rare that villagers ignored their possibility and would not admit it even to their thoughts.[3] Widows who remarried were never again the same in the eyes of the community, no matter how long the interval of mourning or the extent of the need.

Supplementing all relationships was the system of godparenthood -- "Il Comparatico". This curious and complicated custom brought persons and whole families into a relationship sometimes stronger than that of kinship. Families had dozens of "compari" in one village. And in the very small villages --paeselli-- it was not unusual for each villager to have some connection with every other. A "compare" and a "comare", godfather and godmother, were selected for a child at christening,

[3]Phyllis Williams, South Italian Folkways (New Haven: Yale University Press) 1938. But some illegitimacy occured among the servants of the rich.

confirmation and marriage. Thus each child of a large family could have
from two to six Godparents.

Godparents took their roles seriously, they were expected to be
the spiritual directors of those to whom they were related by the
solemn bonds of church ceremony. Originally it was believed that children
even inherited the moral attributes of their godparents. Always welcome
in the homes of their charges, they enjoyed a unique role of authority
which at times superseded even that of the father. The "comparatico"
thus strengthened the stability of Italian family life in South Italy.

This pattern was brought to Newark in fragments. Few families
migrated as a unit, primarily because the expense was prohibitive.
Before burning all bridges behind them, families preferred to wait for
the American reports from the member who played the role of scout.

As the immigrants found work, saved money, and sent for parents,
wives, children and betrothed, the fragments were gradually fitted
together until the ancient family form was reestablished in the new
environment.

As the colony grew, young workers seeking wives again had recourse
to the "masciata". This resurrection enjoyed an even greater success
here, facilitated by the zealous desire of Italian immigrant girls to
be "sistemate" and thus to dissipate the nostalgia and loneliness of
emigration in the joys and responsibilities of family life. So
successful was the Newark version of the "masciata" that it lingers to
this day, but only as a pallid survival, a touching reminder of the
security of love and marriage in a world which is rapidly adding

emotional to economic insecurity.[4]

There were, of course, many exceptions to this pattern, arising from chance encounters and traditional romantic attractions. Such deviations are typified by the account given to an interviewer by a housewife who came here from the province of Salerno at the age of sixteen. Arriving in Newark in 1896 in the company of her sister and a brother-in-law, she had left behind an aged, widowed father to whose misfortune had been added the failure of his bootery, which made shoes "only for gentlemen". Unhappy and homesick, she lived in a dreary flat on Drift Street opposite a stable.

One day as she was looking out the window she noticed an old Italian peasant woman looking up at her from the sidewalk. She smiled to the old woman, who within a few minutes had knocked on her door and entered her room. According to the Salerno housewife, the old woman "without the slightest ceremony" announced: "I think you would make a fine wife for my son who is looking for a good woman. He is a hard worker. May I bring him to see you."

Next day the old woman brought her son, who invited the narrator to a "nice cafe" in New York. A month later they were married and took his mother to live with them somewhere in the Ironbound. The respondent concluded her tale with a smile, declaring that she was very happy and that "God had been kind to her and her family since the marriage."

Despite the observable example of slightly different family customs, the father remained lord and master of the household, his wife his

---

[4]A far more common method at present, well understood by the participants, is for a relative of the man to make innumerable visits to the girl's household in order to sound out the receptivity of the girl and her parents.

obedient companion, and the children joyful acquisitions who, however, were to be taught early the virtues of respect and hard work.

At first such a pattern of family conduct was rather parallel to the mores of a sober, Protestant native citizenry. The inevitable conflicts were to come with the appearance of the second generation, who attended Newark's public schools, played in the streets of the city with children of various backgrounds, and worked in the city's factories. For the American-born offspring of the immigrant families, the public school was a new world whose influences were to mold the thoughts and feelings of an entire Italian-American generation in Newark. This process was not only to give them a peculiar consciousness of themselves as hybrid products with uncertain roots in an American world they knew and understood vaguely, and in an Italian world which was even more strange and distant to them. This "self-consciousness" was to be directed, not in a mold of rebellion -- this was to come in an attenuated form later -- against the standards, "ideas" and values of their parents, until the desired conformity with what was considered the "American Way" was achieved.

These boys and girls sat beside "American" children of different appearance and better dressed than themselves. Confirmation of this can be found in Marzulli's book, wherein he deplored the general unkemptness of the colony's school children and urged Italian mothers to use "more soap and water", since in America the one was plentiful and the other free. The class-room neighbors of these young Italo-Americans, already referred to as "Americans", usually, of course, were the offspring of assimilated Irish, English and German immigrants. To these schools the Italian-American pupils brought their long family names, pronounced with difficulty by prim school teachers to the amusement of tittering class rooms. Many, because of family poverty, shined shoes or sold newspapers after school. The understandable cruelty of school mates, coupled with the "Americanization" program of the school authorities, fed this disturbing sense of loss and isolation between the two cultures. References by many educators to the alleged shortcomings of their parents, the glorification of Anglo-Saxon contributions to American beginnings and development made by the school history text-books as compared to those made by Columbus and early Italian navigators (usually referred to as Venetian or Genoese left their impress on minds anxious for complete and unequivocal assimilation. At home the children began to speak English principally and to register an impatience at, if not contempt for, the family's Italian dialect. The gradual appearance of bilingualism was the genesis of the division to take place in the general realm of family problems or at least the outward and visible symbol of the conflict of the two cultures.

This division found expression in parental opposition towards what they considered the excessive freedom of "American Ways" and the opposition of the offspring to their parents' severity, which they looked upon as an obstacle to Americanization. Since the parents at best were ill-equipped to deal with the questioning and complaints of their children, they had recourse only to the ancient tradition of absolute paternal authority which would brook no radical change or nonconformity. Moreover, there has been no exclusive, specially staffed Italian social agency to deal with problems rising from conflicting adjustments.

Consequently, the young Italian-American generation, especially the girls and young women, was raised in what seemed to American observers an atmosphere of elaborate and extensive restrictions. This tended to give them a status of social inferiority in the eyes of their contemporaries, and a whole legend was built up about the "strictness" of Italian families.

Nevertheless, the early family unit of Newark Italian-Americans, rooted as it was in the strong traditions of the old country, survived fairly well the disintegrating impact of American urban life even beyond the First World War. With the depression of 1929, however, unemployment, poverty and relief began to disrupt this unity. This does not mean that the Italian-American family structure crumbled at the first onslaught. The economic breakdown did, however, open a branch through which new ideas filtered and remained, finding ready allies among a generation grown older in years and understanding and more confident in itself and its aspirations. Parents, too, in many instances, had unconsciously succumbed to direct American influence.

The effects of the past decade can be inferred from the fact that Italian families constitute 42 per cent of the foreign-born population on relief in Newark. This percentage, reached in 1937, has held with minor variations from the beginning of the 30's.[5] Additional insight is afforded by the records of the Domestic Relations Court of Essex County, where an American of Italian extraction, Felix A. Forlenza,

---

[5]Characteristics of the New Jersey Relief Population as to Population and Race on November 30, 1937 (1939 Work Projects Administration, Project #665-22-3-14).

now sits as judge. Italians of all generations form 15.1 per cent of population in Essex County, and the percentages of Italian domestic relations court cases in 1928, 1933, and 1938 were respectively 19.3, 16.0 and 18.1.*

A similar relation exists for the Jews. German families, however, have a lower proportion in relation to their population, which is almost equal to that of the Italians. Since these three groups share the tradition of a strong, well-knit, patriarchal family life, the lower German percentage can only be explained by the Germans' much longer stay in America and their more rapid assimilability in contrast to Italians and Jews. Most of the Italian cases involved nonsupport; Italians generally are reluctant to publicize domestic difficulties of a non-economic nature, seeking advice of relatives, "compari" or close friends.

Another index of the difficulties of maintaining a home in the depressed thirties may be seen in the record of tax foreclosures for the years 1930, 1935 and 1939. The peak occured in 1935. National origins were classified by names on the tax foreclosure lists. This system obviously is open to considerable error, but the main outlines are believed valid. Of a total of 1,525 foreclosures in these three years 481 or about 31 per cent were Italian as compared with 291 Jewish, 185 Germans, 53 Polish, 106 Irish, 27 Ukrainian, and 388 other. The tragedy of these figures lies in the intense attachment to a home of his own which is characteristic of the average Italian. As soon as possible a down payment is made on a cheap little structure which may violate the standards of many other Americans but is his where he may reign as master.

Despite, then, the inroads made by the centrifugal forces of Amer-

*See Appendix VII

ican urban life such as autos and movies and the constantly increasing
tendency to seek interests outside the family circle, Italian-American
family life in Newark offers few alterations in composition and concepts,
but these changes are significant and important.

A survey conducted among 391 Italian families of the first generation showed a mean average of 4.2 children per family, while for 336
second-generation families it was only 2.4. While this tendency towards
family limitation is nearly universal, so drastic a drop is especially
significant when it concerns a group famous for its fecundity and joy
in children, in good times or bad.

In the same groups questions regarding preferences in marriages,
on the whole, indicated no prevalent desire for assimilation. The
overwhelming majority of the 391 persons of the first generation preferred to marry Italians. Peoples of Northern Europe such as Germans,
English and Scandinavians came next in preference. Jews, Negroes
and Orientals were definitely excluded from their choice. Although the
336 respondents of the second generation manifested a general rise in
the degree of tolerance toward other groups in matrimonial matters,
here, too, was clearly indicated first preference for Italians,
secondly for North European groups and the total exclusion of Jews,
Negroes and Orientals. Curiously enough, 3 of the first generation and
1 of the second generation group preferred not to marry Italians. Since
we can assume that in Italy there was no basis for the development of such
strong attitudes against the other groups specified, it must be concluded that such reactions are reflections of what are considered

to be general "American" likes or dislikes.[6]

Despite the factors which tend to disrupt Italian-American house-
holds, the basic family unit promises to survive by far the general dis-
integration of American family life portrayed and prophesied by competent
authorities. This survival will in a large measure be due to the
"restrictions" for which Italian families have become famous. The
social life of the children, especially the girls, remains under strict
supervision, and preoccupation with things and affairs outside immediate family life and interests are still discouraged.

A cardinal principle with most Newark Italian-American families is
that the place of children is in the home until marriage. The common
phenomenon of youths in other families leaving home to seek employment
or better opportunities in a different city is rare. It is considered
a disgrace for a son or daughter to leave the home of his parents and
a reflection on the order and dignity of the family. This deep-rooted
prejudice was also an obstacle to Italian youths going off to college,
but in time it was solved by taking advantage of Catholic institutions
where they felt the religious discipline and atmosphere would surround
the student with the appropriate controls which the family could no
longer exert. Newark Italian parents also feel that their children
should spend vacations with them. Many of them cannot understand a son's
or daughter's desire to vacation alone or with friends, and usually
attribute such a wish to an unwholesome purpose. Until not so long ago
even the Boy Scouts were looked upon with distrust, but now that

[6]See Emory S. Bogardus, Immigration and Race Attitudes (Boston:
D.C. Heath and Company, 1928), p. 25.

Catholic troops have been formed, many Italian boys have convinced
their parents of the advantages of scout membership and occasional out-
door life.

However, this severity in the matter of family, social and individual mores has also produced undesirable results. It has limited the
participation of Italian-American girls, particularly; it has in some
cases produced special hardships by curtailing their social contacts.
Added to this is the exaggerated notion of non-Italians regarding the
"seriousness" of Italian girls. This legend also extends to Italian
youths, who tend to seek associations with non-Italian girls from
whom they expect no serious complications. Thus the average Italian
girl, deprived of the "masciata", also has to undergo relative isolation
from the male world in comparison with her non-Italian sisters. This
situation promises a solution only in the emerging third generation,
whose general outlook and mores will probably not differ much from those
of a typical American community.

CHAPTER VIII

RELIGION AND THE CHURCH

The religion of most Newark Italians retains deep and proud roots in the Italy which was the ecclesiastical mistress of the medieval world and is today the world center of Roman Catholicism.

Since the break-up of the Roman Empire, the Catholic Church in Italy has consciously extended its action to the provinces of government and political activity. This worldliness, skillfully blended with the opposite quality during the Middle Ages, enabled it to hold undisputed sway for centuries in western Europe, particularly in Italy.

The decline of feudalism, the rise of capitalism and the early nationalisms, and the French Revolution in the Eighteenth Century, representing as it did the victory of bourgeois secularism over clericalism, in turn and increasingly limited the extent of the Church's power and prestige.

Left only with Italy, the Church intensified and extended its spiritual and temporal domination of the peninsula, sharing power with kings, dukes and petty princes, when it could not fully control them. Particularly was this domination and prestige well-intrenched in the Kingdom of Naples and Sicily from which the majority of Newark Italians were to come. Here priests, monks and nuns were numerous and powerful in the cities, villages and hilltowns. Religion, particularly in its outer and social manifestations, was a dominating factor in everyday life. Hostile to what it termed "new ideas", the Church did little to lift the veil of superstition and the weight of illiteracy and backwardness which characterized the life of the people.

The social life which is a characteristic of Italian churches in America was not a part of the Italian scene. Except in the large cities, particularly in the North, such activities as dancing were frowned upon by the Church. There were secular groups in the churches known as confraternita, but their activities consisted largely of accompanying the dead on their journeys to the grave and at times helping in public calamities.

In the years following 1870 the church which had always strenuously opposed the long-delayed national unity, was beset by a triple threat from: a secular State acting on an anticlerical middle and land-owning class hungry for the vast Church lands; a growing and militant Socialist Party desirous of liquidating Church authority over industrial and agricultural workers; and a modernist reform movement within the very bosom of the Church, seeking to reform and attune the sacred institution to modern needs.

When speaking of the Church in Italy, the educated Italian shows a mixture of pride and cynicism. Of course, at present there is a tendency to defend Italian institutions which are non-political, and thus to compensate for the world attitude toward Italy. This attitude makes it difficult to dissociate the ideal from the real in discussing the Church in Italy. It seems that after the unification of Italy the educational qualities of the Italian priesthood showed a change for the better. One Newark Italian scholar explains that the temporal dividing

line between the ignorant type of village priest characteristic of South
Italy and the newer educated priest in the same area is about 1890.
This date shows the effects of the new policy of training, which the
Church insisted on after 1870. This change, however, did not mean that
the older, more ignorant priests were entirely displaced; only deaths
and retire ents thinned them out.

Such was the religious situation in Italy at the time when Italians
en masse began to emigrate to America.

Few Catholic Churches existed in Newark at the time of the arrival
of Italians. Mainly German in composition, the Catholic hierarchy of
the New Jersey diocese, under bishop Wigger, was just then laying the
foundations for the spiritual accomodation of the thousands of Catholic
immigrants from all parts of Europe.

Italian immigration in general had always presented peculiar problems to Church authorities, both Catholic and Protestant. Frequently
Church writers of all sects have expressed surprise and wonder over the
earlier Italian immigrant's neglect of the Church and religion in
America. This was attributed severally to the cessation of family
vigilance and social example, primary preoccupation with material welfare,
and the sudden realization that in America the Church and its priests
were not as influential as in Italy. But even when the will to worship
in the ancient faith existed, there were no Italian churches with
Italian priests immediately available.

In Newark, a city founded by English Protestants, Catholic Italians
who sought to observe their religious customs disproved the alarm of
Catholics and the saugness of Protestant phrophecy by crowding the Sunday

morning services in old St. John's Hall on Mulberry Street, on the site
now occupied by the Diocese Building, where Bishop Wigger established an
Italian Mission in March 1882. Here they were ministered to first by the
Rev. Albergo Vitola and later by Rev. Conrad M. Schoetteffer, a German
who was sent here from Rome in 1886 and spoke the Italian language
fluently.

Of this Mission the Newark correspondent of the New York Freeman's
Journal under date of July 2, 1882, wrote: "The Italians are a peculiar
people and the habits and customs of their native land they would transplant in this country: but in time they will learn better. They are not
proverbial for generously supporting the Church, and some seem to think
that they can at will discharge the priest whom the Bishop has sent to
them and supplant him with another of their own selection. Shortly
after the Mission was opened no less than three Italian priests were
invited by their countrymen to come to Newark. These people would like
to own a church edifice, to do with as they please, but they, some of
them, will hesitate long before undertaking a proper share of the
financial burden."

The steady growth of the Newark Italian community in the 80's
rendered acute the problem of the Italian Church, since St. John's Hall
could not accomodate them all. In 1887 Rev. Schoetteffer, in conjunction
with leading Italians, started the Italian quarter on a fund-raising
campaign which resulted in the construction of the Church of St. Philip
Neri, Newark's first real Italian church. The cornerstone was laid in
1887, and in the following year Italians from all parts of the city
joyfully crowded the first service which was celebrated by Schoettefer,

assisted by other New Jersey Church dignitaries.

The Church of St. Philip Neri is on Courthouse Square. People trudging up the hilly portion of Market Street leading to High Street often marvel that a sign post perched on the ground of a Protestant Church directs the passers y to St. Philip's next door. This sign not only indicates the beginning of religious tolerance but is also a pointer to one of the most interesting Catholic churches in the city.

The Church of St. Philip Neri is a two-storied brown brick structure, topped by a squat wooden steeple. It bears a resemblance to an old New England town hall. Sombered by the dust of decades, the old building and the school and rectory adjoining it blend effectively with the atmosphere of red-bricked Court House Square, which, though now an almost forgotten byway, is one of Newark's earliest thoroughfares.

It is the interior of the church, however, which best expresses its quaint character. In the lobby are two wooden stairways leading to the second floor, where services are held. Here the few small arched windows, decorated with colored religious illustrations, produce an effect of intimacy and isolation. On the wall directly above the main altar can be seen the Church's most interesting religious and artistic possession. This is a huge, brilliantly colored fresco of St. Philip, painted by the present pastor of the Church, Father Anthony Alonia, who according to himself "dabbled in art" at the theological school in Rome where he studied. The fresco is a sweeping conception of St. Philip in the role to which Church tradition assigns him -- patron saint and protector of children. Dressed in a heroic crimson robe, St. Philip is shown kneeling in a large patch of blue cloud, his face uplifted.

Above him are winged cherubim; below in the deep background is a miniature but realistic reproduction of the Church and Basilica of St.
Peter's in Rome. In the foreground three small boys in modern dress
look upward to St. Philip, their costumes contrasting sharply with the
Saint's traditional flowing robes. Father Alonia explained his
treatment: "I wished to stress the role of St. Philip for modern children.
It is very necessary."

Father Alonia was appointed to this church in 1937. Born near
Palermo, Sicily, in 1906, he came to America in 1926. After graduating
with a degree of philosophy from the Gregorian University in Rome,
Father Alonia became a member of the famous society of Pallottini
Fathers, forerunners of modern Catholic Action. Ordained in Baltimore,
he became assistant pastor of Our Lady of Mt. Carmel Church in New
York City in 1929, where he remained until his transfer here.

Today Father Alonia, the capable and cultured pastor of Newark's
first Italian church, is fighting a slow and losing battle against
forces over which he has no control. Father Alonia explained that
"our Italians, Genoese, Neapolitans, Sicilians are moving from here."
He attributes this to construction of the new courthouse and the
consequent commercialization of the area. Now the parishioners number
about 500. The drop in membership has not affected the affection of
old timers for the parish, however; for in September 1938 nearly all
of them returned to celebrate the Church's Golden Jubilee. Under
Father Alonia's pastorate the Holy Name Society and the Children of
Mary Sodality have increased in membership, as has attendance at the
church school. During the fifty-odd years of its existence, the church

has performed 1,1335 marriages and 7,170 baptisms. Four Masses are said
every Sunday, and one on Wednesday and Friday. There is also an annual
Novena to Our Lady of the Miraculous Medal.

Our Lady of Mt. Carmel, the second Italian Catholic Church, was
established at McWhorter and Ferry Streets for the benefit of those
Italians who live in the River Street colony and those who have spread
in large groups throughout the Ironbound area. In 1890 the Rev. Alex-
ander McWhorter sold his cement-stoned Second Reformed Church to
Italian Catholic interests -- a tacit admission of the native Protestant
evacuation and the Italian occupation of the "downneck" area.

The first pastorship of Our Lady of Mr. Carmel was entrusted to
the Rev. Conrad . Schoetteffer. He was followed by the Rev. Joseph
Ali, Jerusalem-born, who had already assisted Rev. Schoetteffer at
St. John's. Father Ali remained until 1894, when Ironbound Italians
received as their new pastor, the Rev. Ernesto D'Aquila.

D'Aquila was born in 1868 at Vinchiaturo in the Province of
Campobasso, a region adjoining the provinces from which most of his
parishioners came. After completion of theological studies at Boino,
he was ordained at Severo in the Province of Foggia. Following his
ordination he taught music and French in seminaries in Egypt and Syria.

It was not long before Our Lady of Mt. Carmel reflected the
organizing ability of the widely traveled pastor. Improvements were
made in the interior of the church, the number of parishioners was
increased and a parochial school established under the direction of the
Mission Sisters of the Sacred Heart. This school was discontinued in
in 1921 to be reopened almost a decade later.

Father D'Aquila's musical talents found expression here. He was
the church organist and organised among the young immigrants a band which
entertained during church feasts. Outstanding among these was the annual
July feast of Our Lady of Mt. Carmel. At one time the area marked for
festivities stretched ten whole blocks from Walnut along Jefferson
through Oliver Street. Now the feast is celebrated in the square facing
the church, or along a stretch of Oliver Stre t in front of the new
mission and church school opened in 1931 under the auspices of the
Pious Fillipino Sisters. A group of Ironbound Italians is at present
conducting a fund-raising campaign to build a new Italian church on
this site, now the center of Ironbound's Italian population.

Father D'Aquila, who became a Monsignor before his death about ten
years ago, was succeeded by the Rev. J. Ruggiero, now pastor of
St. Lucy's Church in the First Ward. In 1933 the Rev. Leonard Viccaro,
the incumbent, was appointed.

Born in S. Mauro Forte, Province of Matera, Viccaro was ordained in
1909. During the World War he served with the Italian army for three
years and came to America in 1923. His first assignment here was as
assistant pastor at the Church of St. Rosario in Jersey City. He
served a Montclair parish for a short time before coming to Newark.

Father Viccaro is the heir of the organizational traditions of the
late Father D'Aquila. One of his most cherished interests is the
Mt. Carmel Parochial School on Oliver Street. Here hundreds of Italian
children receive religious and secular instruction from the Pious
Fillipino Sisters. The school pursues a vigorous policy of imparting
to Italian-American children a knowledge and love of the Italian language.

Viccaro is a frequent visitor to the school and often assists the teachers in their work. Italian is taught not without a mixture of politics, as can be inferred from the following verse learned by the children: "Uno, due a tre. Viva il Papa, Il Duce ed Il Re!"[1]

Constructed in the partisan Church pattern, Our Lady of Mt. Carmel has with the years undergone two architectural modifications, one forced upon it by nature, the other a planned alteration which took place in 1935. The cement steeple, shattered by a lightning bolt about fifteen years ago, was never rebuilt to its original height. The present one of wood is a short, domelike structure on the top of which is perched a neon-lit cross. The more recent alteration involved the construction of two massive cement pillars in front of the church, giving it the appearance of a temple.

The interior is decorated in the traditional Catholic manner. The place of honor above the main altar is occupied by a garlanded statue of Our Lady holding the Child. In the rear of the right row of pews stands a statue of Joan of Arc holding aloft a sword. The ceiling is imposingly high and artistically decorated with angelic figures and cherubim, giving a preview of paradisaical bliss to the faithful. These ceiling frescoes of reputable artistic merit were the work of Giovanni Marcantonio Petti, a bizarre immigrant who broke all the traditions of his calling by dying of overeating.

Masses are offered at the church daily and Sunday. The parish house is also the center of numerous religious societies and clubs

[1] In 1939.

for the young and old of both sexes.

The year 1900 saw the establishment of two other Italian Catholic Churches, each rooted in the center of populous Italian districts, the First and Fourteenth Wards.

St. Lucy's Roman Catholic Church was built originally of wood on its present site, 11-13 Sheffield Street. The modest structure represented the sacrifice and activity of leading First Ward Italians under the guidance of the late Monsignor Joseph Perrotti, its first pastor. In 1925, thanks again to the energetic activities of Mgr. Perrotti, the present edifice was built in response to the increasing religious needs of the neighborhood. The present St. Luc 's Church is of solid gray brick in traditional Roman Church design. The simple, whitewashed interior contains many statues of saints and wall frescoes depicting New Testament events. Of particular interest are the two marble statues of the Blessed Virgin and St. Lucy placed on the main altar, which rests between two alcoves in which are smaller altars and statues. Here, too, is the statue of St. Gerardo, miracle worker amongst the sick and afflicted, who has a devoted following of Newark Italians.

St. Gerardo was an illiterate who served the Redemptionists order in Caposelese, Avellino. The large group of Avellino migrants in Newark raised him to a very high position in the activities of Newark Italians. His feast day, September 16, is the beginning of a giant three-day celebration in front of St. Luc 's Church attended by local parishioners and thousands of Italians from outlying towns. The high point of the ceremony is the removal of the statue of the saint and its return after each of the three daily processions.[2]

The feast of St. Gerardo offers an interesting example of the acculturation of Newark's Italians. The street on which St. Lucy's faces is cluttered with booths gaily wrapped in bunting. Here are sold Italian delicacies including various kinds of sausages, nuts, candies, etc. A small carnival is set up on a neighboring street with amusements of several kinds including some mangy-looking circus animals. The stands are run by New York concessionaires who travel around the east exploiting affairs of this kind. However, there are some local booths run by enterprising Newarkers who see a chance to add an honest dollar to meager incomes. A somewhat restrained carnival spirit pervades. The very old sit in rows in a chapel of their church, praying for favorable consideration through St. Gerardo. The more Americanized, after paying their respects to the Saint, repair to the gossip and good feeling of the festival. Children play loudly and swiftly. At intervals the church fife and drum corps returns from its parade through the streets and performs in front of the stand erected before the church. The corps is by no means restricted to Roman Catholic hymns. Particularly striking is the enthusiasm, as portrayed by repetition, for that famous Protestant hymn, "Onward Christian Soldiers".

At night colored lights illuminate the scene, while working men and their wives, restrained by their respective tasks during the day, throng the streets and listen to church dignitaries and Italian politicians speaking from the stand. Occasional side trips to the

[2]In 1941 the statue was not carried through the streets.

numerous bars are made by the men where vino is the drink of the older
ones and beer holds the attention of the young. A tasty roast pig's
head may add to the gustatory delights, varied by a lamb's head seasoned
to taste, or free tripe in a tomato sauce. Salami may be purchased,
or a slice of provalone cheese.

Monsignor Perrotti, who received his title from Bishop J.Walsh
several years before his death, was a beloved and important personality
in Newark's First Ward. His death was widely mourned by thousands. A
special shrine to his memory has been erected by grateful parishioners
in the Holy Sepulchre Cemetery.

Monsignor Perrotti was succeeded by the present pastor, the
Rev. A. Ruggiero. Under his supervision, the Sacred Heart Sisters
conduct an orphan asylum for one hundred orphans in a large modern
building in the rear of the church. The basement of the church, too,
is frequently used as a children's center providing recreation and
religious instruction. In the summer children play in the adjoining
gardens, which has miniature fountains colorfully illuminated at night.

St. Rocco's Church, in the heart of the Fourteenth Ward at
Hunterdon Street and Fourteenth Avenue, is one of the most beautiful
Catholic churches in the city. Its present pastor is the Rev. Umberto
Donati, nationally famous among Italian-Americans.

Established in 1900 as an Italian Mission by the Rev. Guiseppe
Morelli, it became a parish under Father Donati in 1918. Under the
pressure of the increasing Italian population in the Fourteenth Ward,
Donati very early realized the necessity of building a new church.
Despite his zeal and ceaseless activity the cornerstone of the new church

was not laid until 1926. Financial difficulties halted any further work for a decade. Undismayed, Father Donati revived fund-raising activities, and in 1937 his enthusiasm and the generosity of the colony found tri-umphant expression in the new Church of St. Rocco. Members of the congregation who were out of work at the time voluntarily supplied their labor.

This handsome building is an exact replica of the church in the city of Landinera, Province of Rovigo, which Donati admired as a youth. Built of buff brick set off with corner angles of white granite and stone in pure Rennaissance style, St. Rocco's Church brings something of the flavor of Medicean Florence to Newark.

The interior, whose high ceiling is supported by many marble-colored columns, conforms to the patterns of beauty and interest set by the church's exterior construction. Three altars of fine Carrara marble are the church's proudest possession. Above the main altar a giant silver crucifix enshrined in the cupola is also of interest, as are the beautifully stained tall glass windows portraying familiar Catholic themes.

Father Donati, born in the Province of Arezzo in 1872, began his theological studies at the age of eight in Florence. He became a priest in 1896. He returned to Arezzo after he was ordained but, according to a biographer, "his energetic character could not tolerate a life of calm, even if spent in holy duties." That year he came to America, where after religious duties in Paterson and Orange, New Jersey, and in North Carolina he was appointed to St. Rocco's in 1918.

The Church of the Immaculate Conception, 796 Summer Avenue,

incorporated in 1925 by the late Bishop O'Connor, was originally the
Italian Mission of the parish of St. Anthony in "Silver Lake". The
church was built from a former movie house as a result of the spread of
Italians throughout the once desolate "Woodside" section. So completely
conventional in the Catholic sense is the interior that all vestiges
of its former profane career are entirely obliterated.

The Rev. F.P. Mastice has been pastor since its formation. Born
in Potenza, Italy, in 1886, he was ordained in 1910. For the war
period he was a chaplain in the Garibaldi Hospital for Veterans in
Naples. He came to America in 1920 and after teaching languages at
the Arlington Seminary and serving as assistant pastor of the Holy
Rosary Church in Jersey City received his present appointment.

There are no Italian bishops in the diocese and never have been.
Higher officials of the Church are usually Irish and sometimes German.
Of the Judices Pro Synodales one of the eleven is Italian and of the
Parochi Consultores only one in ten. This in spite of the fact that
Italians have as many parishioners as any other ethnic group. Although
all of the Italian churches have Italian pastors, four of them have
non-Italian assistants. The minor influence of Italian priests in the
larger offices of the Church may be due to their foreign birth and
late entrance into the diocesan hierarchy.

Protestanism, despite numerous Italian forerunners such as the
Twelfth Century dissenter Arnaldo da Brescia, never took deep root in
Italy, since it had the support of no important social class. Through
the centuries the movement, working often under difficulties, has
generally met with indifference from the Italians, who tend to choose

between the extremes of Catholicism or atheism. Few Italian Protestants
imigrated to this country. There are no records indicating that any
were among the city's first Italians.

Among the early immigrants, however, there were some converts to
Protestant creeds. In contrast to his sharp criticism of Italian
Catholics in Newark, Marzulli wrote: "Protestant ministers despite
their persistent efforts and propaganda, have not succeede in winning
many proselytes among our co-nationals. In truth, the Italian Protestant
element is more intelligent and under aspects even more respectable than
the Catholics. Protestants, it is known, do not abandon themselves to
those religious orgies known as processions. They have a greater spirit
of tolerance and are animated by humanitarian sentiment."

The few Italian Protestant Churches in the city at present are
the struggling outgrowth of very humble beginnings, usually unused stores
where half a dozen converts and a zealous traveling minister read and
studied the Bible together. They usually have a melancholy appearance
although they manage to carry out a limited religious and recreational
program.

The oldest of these in the city is Olivet Chapel, Hunterdon Street
and Fourteenth Avenue. It was established as a mission in 1903, in a
small store at 52 Fourteenth Avenue, under the supervision of the
First Italian Presbyterian Church in New York. An influx of converts
and new members necessitated the construction of the present Gothic
wood and stucco edifice, opened in 1906 under the pastorship of the
Rev. J. Coltorte, who succeeded the mission pastor, the Rev. Faranello,
when he returned to Italy. The church has at present 208 members, while

458 children attend the Sunday School. In addition to regular services there are meetings of clubs and groups of both sexes in the parish house.

The First Italian Baptist Church, 75 Park Avenue, also began in a store, from which it moved into a frame building until the present pleasant brick structure was built in 1905. Its current membership is less than 95. Two women missionaries conduct Sabbath services and sponsor frequent socials.

In the ironbound area the modest cement-stone structure of the First Italian Presbyterian Church, Jefferson Street between East Kinney and Oliver Streets, was established in 1909. It has a membership of almost 200 converts among neighborhood Italians. The present pastor, the Rev. Bartolini, conducts services weekly.

In general Newark Italians remain attached firmly to the predominant faith of the old country. Although many, because of indifference or the pressure of other interests, do not attend a church or participate in its activities, few acknowledge no faith whatsoever. Most Italian priests express themselves as satisfied with church attendance and pleased with the interest manifested by their parishioners. Some, however, deplore the consequences of church finances due to unemployment, poverty and relief standards.

This general observation, seconded by statements of Italian Catholic Church authorities, was substantiated by a survey in the principal Italian sections in the summer of 1938. Of 354 male and female Italians of the first generation, 341 gave their religious affiliations as Catholics. None admitted being aethists, free thinkers or nonconformists in the matter of religion. Of 244 of the second

generation, 231 acknowledged Roman Catholicism as their faith. Only
13 declared a form of Protestantism as their religion, while none were
atheists, free thinkers or nonconformists. All but a score of the two
groups were from provinces south of Naples.

Of the 341 acknowledged Catholics in the first generation, 305
attended church: 150, occasionally; 102, weekly; 15, once a month;
5 more than once a week; 15, daily. In the second group, of the 231
Catholics, 207 attended: 144, occasionally; 55, weekly; 7, once a
month, and only 2 more than once a week. None admitted attending church
daily.

On the basis of the survey it appears that the church faces no
youth problem among Italian-Americans. Despite the prophecies that the
distractions and diversions of American life would mean the weaning away
of Italian youth from the faith of their fathers, no such development
is immediately discernible. On the contrary, the prolonged economic
depression and the consequent material and spiritual insecurity has
resulted in something of a religious revival among Italian youth. This
is evidenced by the growth of Holy Name Societies in the various Italian
parishes and the greater participation in social activities sponsored
by youth societies of the various churches.

However, the Catholic Church in Newark, as well as in America, is
confronted with one problem regarding young Italian-Americans. This
lies in the reluctance of Italian-Americans to enter the priesthood,
despite frequent exhortations and numerous encouragements and inducements.
Many Italian-American girls, however, have taken the veil. The
inevitable disappearance of Italian-born priests leaves the Church in

America faced with a problem the seriousness of which cannot be overlooked.

The superstitions of the old country die very slowly. Although the old practices are atrophying and some are almost gone, there remain fairly large groups, especially in the old generation who believe in them. In general there are two types of old beliefs; those associated with the saints; and pagan practices of the old religions of southern Europe on which Christianity had been superimposed.

Perhaps the most widespread is the belief in the evil eye - malocchio - pronounced by the peasant without the last syllable. Other terms much less used are oocule, malegni, and jettatura. Sartorio points out that all Italians of whatever generation know something about it. At least partial credence is given to it by the second generation.[3] The influence of the evil eye on children is especially dreaded. Ill-health and ill-luck may be attributed to the influence of "the eyes." Various stories are current in Newark and, other investigators report, elsewhere in America, of cases either here or in Italy where "the eyes" have been the cause of sickness or ill-luck. One such is the story of the man who acted as godfather three times and all the children died. He was credited with the evil eye and avoided by fearful mothers and their children.[4] D'Angelo mentions the incidence of "seers and poets" in Abruzzi. Old women made precarious livings by visiting various homes

[3] Rev. Enrico Sartorio, Social and Religious Life of the Italians in America (Boston: Christopher Publishing House, 1918), p. 100.

[4] Encyclopedia of Superstition (Chicago: J.H. Yewdale & Sons, 1903), p. 25.

where they were well treated because of the fear of the evil eye or some form of witchcraft.[5] This idea is still widespread among the Newark Italians.

There are various charms which may be used to ward off the evil eye. In Italy jet beetles protected against the evil eye as did several other articles made of jet.[6] Many amulets are credited with the power to nullify the potency of the evil eye. Particularly prevalent is the use of coral or sometimes silver, gold, bone, or wing symbols in the shape of horns, teeth or claws. Cornecelli, or little horns, are the most used. Scissors held open, knives, and male hunchbacks help ward off the effects. These charms have been observed almost anywhere around the house. Young infants in particular in Newark are apt to have one type of amulet or another pinned to them. Detection of those under the spell of the evil eye is achieved by dropping olive oil on water. If it remains together the evil eye is at work. It is necessary then to dispel the evil influence by cutting the oil with a scissors or knife while reciting a charm or repeating, "In the name of the Father, the Son, and the Holy Ghost." This phrase may also be said in detecting the evil eye.[7]

The incidence of witchcraft and magic of various kinds is much less noticeable. It is, therefore, harder to find examples. As Sartorio says there are magicians, male and female, who are recipients of appeals

[5] Pascal D'Angelo, Son of Italy (New York: The Macmillan Company, 1924), p. 25

[6] Sir E.A. Wallis Budge, Amulets and Superstition (New York: Oxford University Press, 1930), p. 311.

[7] Phyllis H. Williams, South Italian Folkways in Europe and America (New Haven: Yale University Press, 1938), p. 142.

from Italians which earn them a living of sorts.[8] Love potions are
concocted and mothers consult these fattucchiera to insure good health
for their children. When doctors have given up loved ones, the maga may
be called as a last resort by a frantic relative. Less and less are
these devices being used due to the sceptical attitude of the more
Americanized. Disgust with such practice by children or husband may be
enough to prevent its use. The more accepted Church comfort is rapidly
displacing these pagan survivals, particularly the power attributed to
the saints.

THE SAINTS

The Saints play a very important role in the religious life of
the Italians. Every little town in Italy had at least one patron saint,
whose protection was counted on by those who came to America. In
addition to these patron saints of whom there are hundreds, there are
many whose powers are so famous that they have widespread followings in
all towns. St. Gennaro is one of these. The story of his canonization
is believed literally by most of the old people and by large numbers of
the young. He was executed by the authorities in a small town outside
of Naples for his teachings. A woman who knew him collected some of
his blood in two bottles. She accidentally noticed that the blood
liquefied on the anniversary of his execution. After checking this
miracle on the next anniversary, she brought the blood to the bishop
who decided it was a miracle, and the process of canonization was begun.

[8]Rev. Enrico C. Sartorio, Social and Religious Life of the Italians in
America (Boston: Christopher Publishing House, 1918), p. 100.

His head was recovered by a fisherman, and the bishop had it goldplated. Each year the relics are displayed and the liquefication is awaited by the populace. A striking attitude characteristic of the Neopolitans is their tendency to vilify St. Gennaro if the expected miracles are not forthcoming. Notable, too, is the tendency of the South Italian to try to strike bargains with the saints. Promises of candles, etc. are made if the saint will grant the favor or intercede with God.

Various saints whose fame is widespread have attributed to them specific interests in various parts of the body. Thus St. Biagio is appealed to for help in the cure of a sore throat, while St. Lucy is the one to ask for aid in any illness of the eyes. Don Bosco, a recently canonized saint, is credited with particular interest in the young. Two saints, St. Jude and St. Rita, are those to whom people in despair may turn. They may help in requests which seem impossible. St. Rocco may be asked to protect devout Italians from the plague. St. Anthony of Padua is believed to make thirteen graces a day to God. Prayers are made to him to intercede with God at one of these graces. All of these saints may be asked to help prevent illness or misfortune as well as to aid during some personal catastrophe. Thus there is a specific day on which the throats of parishioners are blessed by the priest whether illness exists or not.

Guardian angels look after each Italian child. They are extremely partisan angels and hide their heads under their wings to prevent seeing any wrongdoing of their charges.

The religious feeling of the Italian is a complex determined by the proportionate parts of first and second generation influences, the extent of anti-clericalism (but not anti-Catholicism), sex factors, Americanization, guilt complexes, ritualistic habits, and a last resource in time of trouble. The deep religious conviction of the first generation is translated in the second generation to habitual duties to the church, with an indefinite percentage retaining the simple faith of their parents. As is usual in all churches, the women and girls are more religious both in their faith and in their observance of duties required by the church.

A number of Italian men and some women have maintained the antipathy to the church organization which they had in Italy. Most of this feeling does not result in lack of faith, but in a dislike for and a suspicion of the activities and intentions of church officials. Add to this number those who were amazed and distressed by the different church conditions of America. Particularly distressing to them was and is the demands of the church for funds, which, compared to the old country, run into enormous sums. They dislike intensely paying for seat money, for example. Then the fees which the church exacts for every activity from birth to death seem excessive to large groups of the first generation, remembering as they do the modest fees of Italy. The result has been that the Italians have a reputation in the general church body for being bad supporters of the church. More penetrating minds in the diocese recognize the reasons for seeming penuriousness of the Italians and place the blame for the misunderstanding on the American clergy who have not done enough to bring the Italians into the community scene.

There was a tendency on the part of the Italian second generation to go to the more Americanized churches. This tendency, however, has been reversed by the purposeful appeal of the Italian churches to young people.

In actuality the Italians of the second generation seem to follow the pattern of large groups of churchgoers in America. That is, they go through the formalities required by the Church and consider their duty done. The approach of trouble, however, sends them to church to appeal to the saints for intercession with God.

In their homes the first generation would be lost without holy pictures in the bedrooms. Usually, too, there is a candle burning in front of a holy picture or a crucifix, particularly after the death of a loved one, or when asking for a special favor. As families are typically large, there is usually some person for whom a candle is burning. Second generation houses, however, show decreasing numbers of holy pictures, down to those who have none. Nevertheless, rare is the house without at least one. Personal prayers are said widely by the old people both morning and night. The young people again do less.

The use of scapulars (scapolare), common to Roman Catholics, is still an essential part of the older people's personal religious observance. Rare was the young man who left Italy without a scapolare, the gift of his mother, around his neck. This custom has become a tradition in America where many Italian children continue to wear these amulets. In the young, however, there is a tendency to replace these with silver medals.

Other aspects of the influence of religion on Newark Italians are associated with modern family and social life and are elaborated in other chapters.

CHAPTER IX

POLITICAL LIFE

The Italians, discriminated against in private industry and, for
a period, excluded from the professions, have found compensation in
politics. Representation of the group through the ballot and in public
office has built up its self-respect. Thrust aside and despised by
Germans and Irish and other earlier immigrant factions, they eagerly
adapted themselves to the intricate machinery of ward politics. Here
they were able to prove their abilities. But first there were
difficulties to be overcome.

In the very early part of the Twentieth Century the United States
and Italy had divergent views on citizenship. The Italian government
held that the children of any Italian subject, no matter where they were
born, assumed the status of the parent. The United States, on the
contrary, contended that the individual must decide for himself.[1] The
early Italian immigrant was, thus, torn between his desire for naturalization and his loyalty to his native land. This dilemma, although not
the strongest, was a determining factor in retarding naturalization.

[1]See speech of former Italian Foreign Affairs Minister, Senator
Tommaso Tittoni delivered in the Italian Chamber of Deputies
March 3, 1905. The speech is found in Senator Tittoni's Italy's
Foreign and Colonial Policy (New York: Dutton, 1914), pp. 168-169.

Census authorities at the turn of the century discovered that as many as 40% of Italian immigrants who had been here for a period of six to nine years failed to declare their intention of becoming citizens. However, only 7% of those who had been here twenty years and more had "retained allegiance to their former governments."

The desire of many first generation Italians was to accumul te money in America and return to Italy, where the American dollar had high value. In 1905 figures show that compared to new arrivals a figure equal to 31% of first generation Italian immigrants returned to Italy for this reason. In 1906, 38% returned; in 1907, 62%; in 1908, 34%; in 1909, 30% and in 1910, 42%. Approximately 15% of these came back to America.*

In commenting upon this aspect of naturalization, Mariano said, "The 'older immigration' represented by the German and Irish stocks have greater political significance because of this, when compared with the 'newer immigration', the Italians, Slavs and Russian Jews. But 7% to 13% of the foreign immigrants are 'aliens and therefore have no influence through the franchise'." The percentage of Italians that are citizens as found by the immigration Commission in a representative investigation some years ago covering more than 8,000 case is given below:**

NUMBER OF ITALIANS WHO ARE CITIZENS

RACE	NO. REPORTING COMPLETE DATA	NO. FULLY NATURALIZED	FIRST PAPERS	PERCENT FULLY NATURALIZED	PERCENT FIRST APERS
North Italian	4,069	1,028	834	25.3	20.5
South Italian	3,811	597	547	15.7	14.3

This percentage of 25.3 true in the case of Northern Italians surpassed the per entages found in the investigation for other numerous

*The Italian Contribution to American Democracy, John Horace Mariano (Boston: The Christopher Publishing House, 1921).

**Ibid, Chap. VIII

immigrants from Eastern Europe." Here is another indication of the difference between northern and southern Italians.

Politics held little or no interest for the early immigrants, concerned with the question of settlement and earning a livelihood. Domestic life, the Church and the jobs occupied their minds and time to the exclusion of things not immediately related to their economic and family needs.

Moreover, there was no tradition of active participation in politics in the homeland, where they were largely disfranchised by voting quali-fications.

Once having settled fairly well the main problems of existence, the Italian became keenly aware of his ignorance of the political life of his new community. He desired to participate in the political arena, but his failure to speak the language of his chosen home greatly limited him. His interest, therefore, turned to political activities in the homeland, celebrated important Italian political events, to which his press directed his attention. Here was the origin of the Italian interest in things Italian merely because they were so. This lack of politial sophistication was to cost them dear.

Another obstacle to the Italian in his quest for political recogni-tion was the retention of extreme regionalism. Comparable to the pre-Civil War state loyalties of Americans, in the case of Italians it extended to towns as well as provinces.

Regional differences were particularly strong in the first genera-tion, showing a tendency to diminish the second. This was most clearly reflected, perhaps, in the inability to agree upon specific leaders.

Marzulli wrote: "The ferocious aversion which keeps families, societies, immigrants from different provinces in a state of war tends to be mitigated only now when the Americanization of Italians is beginning. But the old generation is an immense obstacle to such transformation. Like the Genoese who have lost every trace of Italianity, the new generation disinterest themselves of all provincial antagonisms, as they are penetrated by the spirit and forms of American Civilization." However dubious Marzulli's assertion that Genoese lose their Italianity, his other remarks were undoubtedly true.

The Italian immigration represented all parts of Italy and a mixed pattern of customs, emotions, viewpoints, and dialects. Those from North Italy, who had enjoyed educational and economic benefits denied to the southerners, were contemptuous of the latter. Throughout the peninsula this "campanilism"[2] made people living in close geographical proximity almost alien to each other. Inhabitants of the South were peasants or small town shopkeepers, and they brought to America a rustic and provincial outlook. Thus they clashed with the more cosmopolitan attitude of their Central and Northern countrymen. These deep-rooted sectional prejudices made it extremely difficult to unite the Italian electorate of Newark.

Growing interest in politics was stimulated as the Italians acquired real estate and became tax-payers. This brought them closer to the City Hall, the Tax Assessor's office and the politicians who operated the municipal apparatus.

[2]Literally within sound of the village church bell - village mindedness.

The analysis by Roberts demonstrates that because they settled here before the Italians, the Irish and Germans were earlier Americanized and naturalized and consequently have dominated Newark's political life for the last 50 years. To the Italians, who came later, naturalization was an uphill fight and political representation involved a struggle against a firmly entrenched Irish and German electorate. Conversely, in South America, where numerous Italians settled at an early date, they form a dominant group.

At the time of the first influx of Italians to Newark the Irish politicians were engaged in a struggle with those of native stock, and they anticipated valuable allies in the Italians. The big obstacle was the illiteracy and noncitizenship of the bulk of the Italian inhabitants. The political machines contrived to attract the Italians by distribution of numerous street cleaning and other low-paid jobs. Strangley, the Italian felt no resentment but for a time pointed with pride to this form of employment. To him it was an obvious sign of citizenship.

The Republican party because of its early entrenchment in local politics enlisted Italian support and has held it with few deviations. The Republicans, through the more astute and articulate members of the Italian colony, were able to plant a system of bossism and ward politics which nourished by an extensive process of patronage became firmly rooted and flourished for many years. The Italians were grateful for recognition no matter how cursory; for a few pleasant words, a pat on the back, or a glass of beer, they were willing to sell their suffrage. To them the Republicans represented security, jobs and Americanism.

McKinley at the turn of the century was their American hero.

Theodore Roosevelt's vigorous liberalism and apparent earthiness especially attracted these energetic people. They felt a kinship with the "rough-rider". His papers, translated into Italian, were widely read.

There have been periodic shifts to the Democratic party but they have brought no permanent change, and returns to the Republican fold have been mechanically consistent.[3]

In the early colony a few socialists attempted to become a dynamic force but their concern with Utopian concepts of both politics and social needs and their failure to face practical problems left them with only meager influence. Their strange dress and rabid anti-clericalism proved very distasteful to the Italian, and they were consistently rejected. Marzulli considered them not genuine apostles of Socialism but rather men who were drunk with the frenzy of their own words but "never drunk with the same courage."

Although the first Italian was recorded in Newark in 1864, it was not until 1876 that one, G.B. Ferrelli, was naturalized. Two years later J. Franoni was elected to the minor post of Justice of the Peace.

The first political organization of Italians was formed about 1878 and dedicated to the Republican Party. Although its membership reached 300, it lasted for a few years and then was liquidated because of religious prejudices. There followed a long list of political clubs on the familiar pattern of ward politics in American cities.

[3]Thus in the presidential election of 1940 Wilkie carried the first ward (normally Democratic), although the Democratic candidate for Governor, Charles Edison, carried the ward.

Politically ambitious men, after serving an apprenticeship as poll watchers, were singled out by the major parties as leaders in their nationality areas. Eventually they formed clubs, often named after themselves. From then on it was a question of retaining the votes they controlled in return for minor political positions.

The local Italian press plays an insignificant role in politics and is not widely read. Throughout its history it has reflected rather than formed the political opinions of its readers. The papers have been concerned with the interests of the Italian group rather than with the larger issues of American life. They have consistently devoted much of their space to exploiting the ambitions of Italians working for political appointments and to applauding their success. The early papers were all Republican, but recently their editorial policy has been nominally independent. In reality they remain not so much Republican or Democrat as Italian, commending the success of co-nationals of either party.

In flowery and extravagant literary style they present their candidates as paragons of virtue while the opponents are pictured as horrible examples of political incompetence and even dishonesty. The editorial policy underlying them all, reduced to its simplest terms, is the glorification of Italians. If no Italian candidate is involved then votes are urged for those who have distributed patronage to Italian-Americans in the past. Larger social questions are neglected. Dedicated to practical politics, the papers usually avoid the extremes of either the conservative or liberal viewpoints. On the whole, they lean to the conservative side. An example of this Italianism is given below.

VOTE FOR GIFFONIELLO AND BOZZA,
ALSO CAVICCHIA AND RODINO

The Italian Tribune is pleased to recommend the election of
Charles C. Giffoniello and Samuel D. Bozza, both candidates for free-
holder of Essex County. The former is a Republican, while the latter is
a Democrat. Three are to be elected.

Fortunately both the Republican and Democratic assembly slates also
contain the names of two Italian-Americans, Dominic A. Cavicchia,
Republican, and Peter W. Rodino, Jr., Democrat. Twelve are to be elected
as members of the assembly from this county.

Republicans and Democrats can vote for these four who are men of
fine character, integrity and well qualified to perform splendid services
for the offices they seek.

We urgently ask our readers to vote for Giffoniello, Bozza,
Cavicchia and Rodino on election day. They are worthy of your support.

Large sections of the first generation are illiterate and thus not
subject to the influence of any newspaper. Those who do read, look to
their paper for news of the local Italian colonies rather than politics
as such.

The large circulations are held by the large New York newspapers,
Il Corriere and Il Progresso, both owned by Generoso Pope. These carry
some New Jersey news but are more metropolitan in outlook. They sub-
scribe to the major news services and have a relatively high standard
of technical efficiency.

Before adopting Commission government, Newark was administered by
a mayor and Common Council. The Common Council, constituted of representatives elected from each district, was similar to the familiar alder-
manic form. The number from each ward was determined by the population,
and each district had at least one representative. The Common Council
governed Newark the latter part of the 19th and the early part of the
20th century. Between 1891 and 1917 Germans and Irish dominated the
council, with a negligible number of Italians and Jews. The Italians
had the smallest representation, despite enormous population growth
which made them in 1940 the largest single national group.*

In 1917 Newark adopted the City Commission form of government, for
which five members were elected at large. This presented the Italian
electorate with new difficulties. Whereas previously the dominantly
Italian wards had been able to elect some candidates, even if they were
so very few, now any concentrated strength, such as in the 1st, 5th
and 14th wards is rendered negligible. From 1917 to 1933 the Italians,
like the Jews, were unable to send one of their group to the City
Commission.

Finally, in 1933, an Italian, Anthony Minisi, and a Jew, Meyer C.
Ellenstein, were elected. In 1937 Ellenstein was reelected, while Minisi
was sixth. In 1933, with 70% of the registered electorate voting, he
carried the 1st and 5th wards again, as well as the 10th and 11th wards.
But in the 9th and 16th wards (heavily Jewish) his vote fell, indicating
perhaps that the past election alliance of 1933 had failed. **

The Italians lobbied strenuously in the City Hall for the selection

*See Appendix VIII
**See Appendix IX

of an Italian-American to fill the vacancy left by the resignation in 1939 of Michael P. Duffy. However, the office was left vacant until the election of 1941, when Ralph Villani, a former judge, was elected with a total of 51,222 votes. He was the sole Republican elected. Also running were Anthony Minisi, Dominick Gennardo, Anthony Giuliano, and Olindo Marzulli. The interesting point is that Villani received the votes of the Ellenstein machine while the Italians of the 1st, 5th and 6th wards did not support Ellenstein. Also interesting is the fact that there were bitter factional feuds between the Italian candidates.

The ineffectiveness of the Italians in securing representation commensurate with their numbers can be attributed to narrow self-interest and sectional differences, plus the wiles of machine politicians who take care to split a vote which might hurt them. Because of loose and unwieldy organization, they have failed to achieve the advantages one would expect from their formidable voting strength.

Naturalization has increased as the group has come to realize that it is an essential to their quest for greater political representation. The new citizens, foreseeing the fruits of political prestige on the horizon, carry on active missionary work to encourage naturalization through education. Where this fails, as it frequently does, they resort to the high pressure technique of ward politics. The first generation has generally succombed to these tactics, and the Italian vote has increased commensurately.

It has been charged that the Italian vote is still under the handicap of prejudice and nationalistic pride which obscures comprehension of the main political issues. This is hardly due to ignorance, as may

have been charged previously, but rather to the persistent and overwhelming desire these people have to be recognised as a social force.
The Italian is inclined to feel that he is still looked down upon by
the so-called "native", and he desires ardently to rise above this lot
by participation in politics. This attitude, rooted in the soil of
emotion, renders him an easy prey to manipulation. In the heat of
controversy his loyalty can be directed as effectively against an
Italian candidate as for him. He responds with enthusiasm to the least
opportunity to gain even superficial recognition through some political
medium. In many campaigns this enthusiasm has attained such a point
that it has swept aside the element of reason, and the Italian electorate
has responded not on the basis of conviction but rather on the promise
that here at last is the opportunity to "rise".

In a survey during 1938-1939 the response to the query, "Would
you like to return to Italy permanently, temporarily or not at all?"
was as follows: of 347 first generation Italians 13 answered permanently, 181 temporarily and 147 not at all, 5 refused to answer. Of
238 Italians of the second generation 3 answered permanently, 113
temporarily, 76 not at all and 46 did not answer. These figures, if
compared with the percentages of 20 and 30 years ago, would reveal a
consistent process of Americanisation. They reveal, too, that a greater
percentage of first generation Italians would like to return to Italy
permanently, which might have been expected. The gap is dwindling,
however.

In the same survey Italians were asked, "Would you like your
children to return to the Old Country, permanently, temporarily or

not at all?" Out of 395 first generation Italians, 2 answered permanently, 176 temporarily, 145 not at all and 72 refused to answer. Of 333 second generation Italians, 1 answered ermanently, 93 temporarily, 79 not at all and 160 declined to answer. This would seem to indicate that in their attitude to their offspring both groups maintain an approach that is consistent with their personal consideration of the homeland.

Out of 392 Italians questioned as to their citizenship, 125 stated that they had not taken out second apers. Of these, when asked if they had taken out their first papers, 33 answered yes, 61 answered no, and 31 failed to answer. On being questioned as to they they had not taken out their first papers, 8 answered for financial reasons, 17 were clearly disinterested, 14 were unable to meet the requirements and 22 refused to answer.

The survey revealed that citizenship is a question of profound importance to the Italian immigrant; that although the first generation Italian may have lived in Newark for a number of years and undergone an intensive process of Americanization, the concept of naturalization in his mind is still surrounded by a series of fears. When he is confronted with the question of citizenship he is apt to view the questioner, in some instances, with suspicion and distrust and even belligerence. In recent years Italian political disunity has been somewhat affected by the achievements of Mussolini in Italy. Pride in Italy's rising prestige has manifested itself in a feeling of national unity but the change has not been so great as to conspicuously alter the course of individual enterprise at the expense of possible collective gain.

Although by far the majority of Italians emigrated before Fascism, their attitudes toward it before the present war were fairly well standardized on a compromise basis. Fully conscious of present American disapproval and even ridicule of Mussolini's Fascism as opposed to American democracy, they had fallen back on an immense pride in Italy's achievements in Europe, especially her ability to rattle the saber and cause respect for her arms. This factor is rooted in a profound conviction that Italy was cheated out of the fruits of victory in 1919 by the machinations of English and French diplomacy. From this low estate Italy has risen to a larger place in European affairs.

Thus although the Italian was a sectionalist at home, he had come to believe in the manifest destiny of today's Roman Empire from his vantage point on this side of the ocean. The Italians in Newark were not particularly Fascistic in their political thinking; in fact few of them could describe the idealogical basis of Fascism. They are just pro-Italian, stemming from their roots in the land of their origin. Had Italy gone Communist after the war, there is little doubt that as many Italians would sympathize with her as now sympathize with Fascism. The point would always be made, however, that they were Americans, and what was good for Italy might not be favorable for America. There is no question as to their patriotism in America. Their attachment to Italy is purely sentimental, while their feeling for the United States is realistic and based on their conviction that America offers them the best opportunities for security and happiness.

There was a great rush of Italian politicians to climb on the

American band wagon with the opening of hostilities between the United
States and Italy. Protestations of the loyalty of Italian-Americans
flew thick and fast. The brutal fact of the war at last made it impossible
to live in an American society and approve of Mussolini. Further, our
Allies, particularly England, must be supported. As nearly as can be
determined the first casualty has been Mussolini. His popularity had
waned progressively with the lack of success of Italian arms: a convenient escape was possible. Now instead of being proud of Italy because
of Mussolini's saber rattling and search for a place in the sun, the
Italians are damning Mussolini for not representing the Italian public.
The potential hurt to Italian pride caused by Italy's continuous
failures as a modern war power is attributed to the lack of enthusiasm
of the Italians for this war. England is not being mentioned, at least
publicly.

As the Italian's attention is being directed to preventing discrimination against him during the war emergency, this has become serious
enough for various groups to issue public appeals for recognition of the
loyalty of Italian-Americans and pleas for no discrimination on defense
jobs.

At the same time developments in world affairs have shown the
emergence of a new set of attitudes. Before the present war first generation Italians particularly were dead set against American participation.
Roosevelt, formerly a popular figure, has lost considerable ground in
the Italian colony. The result has been bitter disputes in the quarter
itself. Their resentment against the administration reached a peak with
the drafting of their sons. Mussolini's famous glorification of war

as part of the Fascist ethics has no place in the heart of Newark's
Italians. A substantial rise in the prestige of the Germans with their
victories in England took place which was followed after the declaration
of war by a reversion to the older attitudes of dislike for the Germans
which oes back to Austrian domination of Italy. Italian politicians
realizing the danger of the situation were very cagey about their
public utterances.

CHAPTER X

ORGANIZATION

The organizational life of Italians is varied and important. In
1938-1939 a total of 225 of their clubs of all kinds were found in
Newark. Most of them are largely social in activities, although established for other purposes. Only 22 were organized frnakly for social
purposes, while 42, based on common origin in an Italian town, are
social in nature. These latter are largely first generation organizations and exist as meeting places where the old guard can gather and
play booce or one of the favorite card games.

The Church sponsors about 20 organizations. The largest and most
influential club in Newark is the Italian Catholic Union of St. Lucy's
Church, organized in 1919 to encourage religious activities and whole-
some recreation. Starting in a basement across the street from St. Lucy's
Church with 12 members, it now occupies a large, modern, three-story
brick building, and has a membership of 1200 men, mostly residents in the
First Ward. The average age was about 32 and whereas all generations are
represented, its program is directed primarily to serve young people.
The present average is 30.

The organization bans all political activity, but has an elaborate
religious, welfare and social program. There is a monthly communion
service, as well as service on Mother's Day and Holy Name Day. A

yearly retreat is conducted in a monastery in Morristown.

Cultural activities include a dramatic group, glee club and lectures on religion and history. Athletics of all kinds are encouraged, including the well-known Gold basketball trounament and softball, track and bowling teams. The Union schedules occasional dances, excursions, and outings for children of the neighborhood.

Several committees assist members in obtaining relief, employment, old age pensions and unemployment compensation. There are, in addition, sick and funeral committees. The organization engages in a variety of charitable activities, such as providing Christmas baskets for the needy. Among its miscellaneous activities the organization carries on considerable work in Americanization.

The physical plant is excellent. On the first floor are bowling and shuffle board alleys, billiard and card tables, showers, locker rooms and a bar. The second floor consists of a meeting room, 42' by 60', convertible into a gymnasium featuring a basketball court and to an auditorium for plays. On the third floor is a library.

There are two classes of membership. The first provides general facilities of the club. The second in addition entitles a member to $10 a week sick benefit for 13 weeks and $7 in the next five weeks as well as a $200 death benefit.

The club succeeds in attracting young men from the streets and unsavory small clubs and has undoubtedly helped reduce the juvenile delinquency and crime rates of the First Ward.

Other social groups, established largely by the second generation,

vary in range of interest from little more than a meeting place of
neighborhood gangs to organisations interested in promoting the social
life of the Italian community and particularly of their own section. The
clubs generally are very small, and all members are known to each other
at least by sight. The Italian tendency to sectionalism is again reflected
in these clubs, which usually draw membership from an area of not more
than four square blocks. Their life as clubs is apt to be extremely
short, and they spring up and decline for no apparent reason.

To illustrate the prevalence of this type of organization, along
7th Avenue of the First Ward, one of the main arteries of a large Italian
colony, are displayed the names of at least 20 within the space of five
blocks. Names taken at random show a wide variety of influences. The
20th Century Club, the Abruzzese Society, The Sunrise Pleasure Club,
The Circolo Flumarese, The Society San Giorgio and similar placards are
seen in the windows of small stores as well as such unaccountable titles
as the Lincoln Highway Social Club and the Martin Van Buren Association.

The social clubs are rather sharply divided into those of the first
generation and those of their children, to provide for as does nothing
else the difference in interest between the two groups. Often the
average member of the second generation spends considerably more money
in these organisations than the family budget can reasonably stand.
Other aspects of the standard of living therefore suffer.

Clubs offer little to the Italian community beside recreation. The
first requisite is a card table where Italian games mingle with American
games to the improvement of neither. In first generation clubs, Italian
games are most popular. Activity, at most, is extended to a dance or outing.

Intellectual activities simply do not exist. There is no unifying force among them which could work f r the betterment of Italian life. The tendency is to remain sectional, small and self-interested.

Some few, such as the Tripoli Social Club, conduct meetings in the parliamentary manner. These may often be converted into political organizati ns.

Memberships are largely made up of unskilled workers, but there are also a number of skilled mechanics and office workers, as well as some lawyers, doctors and public officials, especially those ambitious of leadership in the Italian community. To the first generation Italian, his club constitutes a large section of recreational life. Here he can express himself fluently in his native tongue and run no risk of ridicule for his accent.

Typical of the soc al club catering to first generation men is the Circolo Dopolavoro, which meets in a store on Warren Street. Its name, meaning "after work", is the same as that of the official workers' recreational organization in Fascist Italy. The president denies any affiliation with the Italian movement and attributes the coincidence in names to a happy inspiration. It was or anized in 1934 by 24 workers drawn from the neighborhood, as is usual for such groups.[1] The president Mr. Rense, is a barber shop proprietor, and the treasurer owns a confectionary store.

Permission could not be obtained to attend a meeting of the club. From the president's statement, however, it appears that members spend

[1] The date of the organization and the fame of the old country's Circolo Dopolavoro are significant.

their time playing Italian card games and bocce. Occasionally, when affairs of great interest to Italians arise, such as the Italo-Ethiopian War, members raise money, food and clothes for the homeland. In addition needy community members are helped occasionally. Over the green shades that cover most of the store windows can be glimpsed portraits of President Roosevelt and George Washington and a variety of paintings of saints on the walls. Signs in Italian proclaim that dues are to be paid regularly and that no strangers are to be entertained on the premises.

Such organizations as these offer a great deal of pleasure to members in their sympathetic interest and their mutual dependence and constitute a refuge for those who have been disinherited by America. They can be duplicated in every Italian colony of the city wherever tenements, poverty and lack of extra funds for recreation make them necessary. Other nationalities have similar organizations although somewhat broader in scope. For example, the Ukrainians and the Poles are likely to form large organizations which are completely equipped or to build large halls to which a considerable portion of the population may forgather for amusement.

At the opposite extreme is the Casa Italiana Social Club, considered one of the most influential Italian organizations in the city. The club is at 211 Littleton Avenue and 14th Avenue, in the center of a large Italian colony in Newark's uptown section. Even its location indicates the higher socio-economic status of the 950 members, comprising men and women from all walks of life. One of the largest of its type, it embodies not only social features but recreational and educational as well.

The members are divided in three groups, which are: a parental

group from which the governing body is selected; a ladies auxiliary and
a youth group which is made up mostly from their sons and daughters.

The parental or older group, which is the greater in numbers,
includes a number of professionals, such as doctors, lawyers, etc., and
members proudly boast that their association is the only one in Newark
which includes in its membership all Italian clerics and all present
or past public office holders, such as former Commissioner A. J. Minisi,
Mayor Bianchi of Orange and former Judge Ungaro Mancuso. It also
includes a large number of Italian war veterans.

Casa Italiana was founded in January, 1938, by a group of Italian
war veterans of whom Dr. Francesco F. Renzulli was a leading figure;
he is still the president. The purpose of the associationwas to promote
Italian cultural and social activities and to foster greater unity among
Italians living in Newark.[2] The educational activities consist of
teaching the Italian language, history and music. The club also has a
large class preparing for naturalization.

The club house is a large wooden colonial structure surrounded by
spacious grounds, providing ample room for the many recreational and
athletic activities which include tennis, baseball, boxing, bocce and
card playing. Fencing is taught by a leading tutor.

The club quarters are excellently maintained. The first level is

[2]The Italian Counsul was also very interested in its founding. Case
Italiane exist all over the world, encouraged by the Italian Consuls.
They are part of the foreign program of the Direzione Generale degli'
Italiani all' Estero.

devoted to the male members; in one room is a modern bar. The second
floor is divided into a number of large rooms in four of which, devoted
to the women's auxiliary, sewing and crocheting are taught. The
remaining rooms are for the exclusive use of the executive body and
directors.

Casa Italiana has succeeded in this organization where most Italian-
American Associations have failed, in fostering close harmony among
Italians from all parts of Italy. A stringent rule is that no political
discussion of any kind is allowed on the premises; violation brings
immediate expulsion. The club is directed by five prominent Italian-
American trustees. Among its members can be found the present, past and
aspiring leaders of the Italian colony.

Although there are 22 mutual aid associations in the Newark Italian
communities, none is large and well financed. Almost invariably the
little paesani groups, which became established early and have endured
to this day, have mutual benefit features, similarly organized. A small
amount is paid to the sick member for a period of 10 or 12 weeks. Very
often medical expenses are also paid. If a member needs additional help
it is customary to take up a collection among the members and non-
member paesani. If he is still unable to manage, a rally or dance is
held at which raffles are run off for his benefit.

Recently there has been an attempt to coordinate these social
groups. The movement has been fostered by the rise of the Sons of Italy,
which has attracted small lodges all over the United States. This
affiliation has brought an extension of benefits as well as a breakdown
of the extreme sectional divisions.

Nationally the Sons of Italy split on the question of fascism; but the New Jersey lodges maintained unity. However, the pro-fascist officers of the original national organization were displaced and there was a return to non-political emphasis.

Of the 22 strictly mutual aid organizations 13 are affiliated with the Sons of Italy. They were organized between 1910 and 1915 with memberships varying from 58 to 70. At present almost all of them have declined in membership. One exception is the Principesa Mafalda di Savoia, named after a daughter of the present king. Organized in March 1914 with 60 members, it has about 85 at present. The average age of the members was 25 when founded but is now 55, indicating a long-time membership. Most of the members are first generation females. The sole purpose is mutual aid, although occasional parties and dances are held, usually to help finances.

Organized similarly in 1915 was a male lodge, Emanuele Gianturco #799. The original membership of 50 with an average age of 30, has now dropped to 40 with an average age of 50. Again all are first generation, working class people. The other lodges have practically identical characteristics. Almost universally they consist of single store front rooms, named after an Italian patriot or personage. Physical equipment consists of chairs and tables. Recent attempts to interest the younger second generation have been conspicuously unsuccessful. The competition of insurance companies has proved too much for the mutual benefit features, and social activities are sufficiently attractive.

Loyalties to both countries are usually symbolized by the display of Italian and American flags and pictures or busts of the current

American president and either Mussolini or King Victor Emanuel or both.

The great interest of Italian youth in sports is reflected in the number of athletic clubs. In all 34 are listed and these are probably only a part of the total. These clubs are usually store front rooms equipped with pool and card tables. Usually they organize baseball, football, and basketball teams to compete with similar clubs of all nationalities.

All of these organizations are second generation and all engage almost exclusively in American sports. The first generation is inclined to frown on their activities as physically dangerous and conducive to loafing. This prejudice is a carryover f the hard physical labor pattern of the old country. The second generation Italian has, however, become a large part of the sporting life of America. Italian boys are attracted to sports as a more pleasant way of making money than by study and preparation for professional or business careers. These clubs place a high emphasis on physical courage and tend to produce boys who develop, or assume, a tough exterior.

Outside of these social and fraternal organizations there are about 72 of political origin. Their political activities, however, are confined to election time. For the remainder of the year they are social clubs.

Lastly there are perhaps 15 or 20 miscellaneous groups such as landbrds' associations, professional or business clubs, cultural clubs and war veterans groups.

The development of a cultural life in a largely illiterate group such as the first generation Italians has been an almost impossible task.

Love of good music they have as a heritage, but other cosmopolitan pursuits have been denied to them. Even in the second generation the lack of advanced education retarded the development of an intellectual group. Even those who took professional training were apt to limit their education to the requirements of their profession and devoted little energy to increasing their knowledge in appreciation of the humanities.

Among Italian-Americans who have sought to broaden the culture of second generation Italians the work of Professor Libero Sibilia, a teacher at Barringer High School, has been outstanding. For the self-consciousness of the Italian boys and girls he substituted a pride and enthusiasm for the native tongue of their parents. He organized student groups to study Italian drama, architecture, paintings and science. A group of the best students was selected to go to Italy to study Roman culture. In addition the Professor has organized I Dilettanti (Junior Order of the Dante Alighieri Society), interested primarily in the drama, an Italian honor society and an Italian Club in the evening high school.

Outside of the schools he has been instrumental in the organization of the Universita Popolare (forum), which now has 50 active members who held forum discussions on many aspects of modern life. Another cultural organization is the Benedetto Croce Educational Society, named after the great Italian philosopher, which is composed of teachers.[3]

The oldest and best known of the cultural clubs is the Dante

[3]The Newark branch was founded about 1932 or 1933 with five or six members. It now numbers between forty and fifty, all men. There seems to be no political connotations to the society whatsoever.

Alighieri Society of Essex County. This organisation invites guest speakers, often Italian Professors at nearby colleges, and holds concerts devoted largely to Italian classics. Lectures are often bilingual. Meetings are usually followed by social hours. The society is also active in forming Italian language classes and in encouraging the teaching of Italian in the public schools.[4]

Strangely enough, a sample of Italians taken in 1939 revealed that very few were willing to admit affiliation with any clubs. About two-thirds of both the first and second generation either refused to answer or claimed that they belonged to no organization. Of those in the first generation who responded, the largest number admitted membership in fraternal organizations with almost as many in religious societies. Membership in trade unions came next while purely national organizations were fourth in popularity.*

It is noteworthy that very few belonged to business and service organizations and none at all to educational organizations.[5]

[4]This organization represents the oldest continuous attempt to perpetuate Italian culture abroad by the Italian government. However, except for the activities of the Italian Consul, who always attended, it seems to have been focused on cultural aims.

[5]The organizational affiliations were difficult to find and were at variance with impressions gained by the staff. These results are believed to be thoroughly unreliable but are presented as we found them.

*See Appendix X

Among those questioned in the second generation, social clubs
and religious societies led the list, while trade unions and fraternal
were almost as popular. The striking differences between the generations in organisational affiliations are revealed by the much larger
number who belong to athletic clubs and service and business groups
plus the negligible number who belong to strictly nationality groups.
Some few in the second generation showed interest in educational organisations.

CHAPTER XI

RECREATION AND SOCIAL LIFE

Most of the formal social activities of first generation Italians are associated with the many clubs composed of fellow townsmen. These clubs have their annual dinners and dances, picnics and feasts.

There are frequent dinners to launch the career of some young professional or to honor a successful conational. The first is apt to be an expensive form of recreation since guests are expected to contribute to a gift, which is frequently a sum of money. Both types of affairs are well organized. A general chairman is assisted by the chairman and members of the arrangements, reception, speakers and publicity committees. The dinner is opened with an invocation by the honored guest's parish priest. A prominent Italian-American is the main speaker, followed by a prominent friendly non-Italian.

Less formally, Italians are known for a hospitality that has become proverbial. "The door is always open", and "there is always enough for one more" are household expressions. Travelers in Italy were received courteously, although with a strong sense of the proprieties. This general attitude has survived in America. A day-time visitor at the home of a Newark Italian, is first offered a drink of cordial, rum or vermouth. Usually, this is followed with some Italian pastry and a cup of black coffee. At mealtime a visitor is always invited to participate without ceremony. The host is insulted if the offer is not accepted or a suitable excuse given.

One of the most enduring types of recreation is the religious festival. Deeply rooted in the tradition of the homeland, it has been little distrubed by transplanting into the new environment. In Italy the ubiquitous religious feast was organized to perpetuate the memory of innumerable patron saints. In the Province of Avellino, for example, there is a religious feast in some town on every Sunday from June 13, the feast of San Antonio, to the first Sunday in october. In Tripaldi alone there are three religious holidays, Madonna Del Carmine, San Antonio and San Sabina.

San Gerardo, who is said to have performed hundreds of iracles, is the patron saint of Caposale, Province of Avellino. any Caposalesi attend St. Lucy's Church, Newark, which has adopted the feast as a parish holiday.[1] Other Italians join in, as well as Caposalesi from distant communities.

Newark's first ward is the scene of unusually gay activity on the 14th, 15th and 16th of October, the feast of the San Gerardo. St. Lucy's Church is beautifully decorated with color-bedecked bandstands flanking the main entrance. The streets in the immediate neighborhood are covered with Italian and American flags and spanned by arches of colored lights. Peddlers with improvised stands line the curbs, displaying Italian confectionary, foods and religious articles. The firework display is continuous.

The high-light of the festival is the three-day religious procession led by a motorcycle policeman and a drum and bugle corps. Next

[1] See chapter on religion.

some girls' and mens' groups. Every section of the ward is systematically covered. As the procession heads into New Street, a series of fireworks is set off to signal to the residents.

The second group is led by uniformed musicians. A lone drummer beating a strange trill on his drum precedes the image of San Gerardo, flanked by an entourage of four altar boys and a priest reading from a Bible.

The procession stops every two or three yards to permit spectators to come to the middle of the street to offer their contribution to a man who recieves the bills and pins them to the garments of the saint. Eventually the head of the Saint can be seen rising above a sea of green dollar bills.

Every day the same procession is followed by about 2,500 women, mostly middle-aged; some are young mothers wheeling their baby carriages. Years ago the women walked barefoot, but today all wear shoes except one white haired woman representing the Society of San Gerardo. She walks in herstocking feet and carries an engraved picture of the saint. The procession comes to an end when the saint is restored to his niche inside the church.[2]

Sampling the population of Newark, it was found that 67 out of every 100 first generation Italians observe some religious holidays, while only 48 per cent of the second generation do so.

The Italian Halloween, "Carnevale", is celebrated here an abroad in much the same manner on the Tuesday before Lent. It is another day

[2]This procession was discontinued in 1940 by order of the Bishop of the diocese. Discernible in recent months has been a tendency for Italians to abandon many of their activities due to a feeling that they should be less conspicuous in these times.

of feasting and fun for young and old. A special cake is made of dried
cod fish, Baccala, and dough fried in olive oil, and served at supper
time.

Reading as a form of recreation was denied to most Italian immigrants
because of the high rate of illiteracy. At first many read romantic
novels and were exploited by booksellers who charged as much as $12
for a paper-covered book sold in installments. These are little read
now.

Difference in language prevents most Italians from enjoying one of
the main American forms of recreation, the movies. Young Italians on
the other hand go so frequently that many parents complain of this
additional American burden.

GAMES

Men engage in numerous games of chance. One of the best known is
"morra" or "throwing fingers". The game, played by two or more people,
usually for drinks, consists in guessing the number of fingers put out
by the opponent and adding them to one's own. "Morra" probably gave
rise to another game which also is played for drinks known as "padrone
e sotto" or "boss and second boss". Drinks are lined up and the boss
offers them one by one to other players. If the second boss approves,
which he never does, the other player drinks; otherwise the boss must
drink. The understood object is to get the boss drunk.

Card games are numerous,"scopa" or "sweep", "tre sette" or three
seven" and "briscola" being the most popular.

In Italy everyone played the government-controlled lotteries.

Usually a veteran acted as agent in the so-called "Banco Lotto". Poor folks who did not see but a few "soldi"[3] a week would play. The "numbers" had to be selected before a given hour on Saturday, and the winning list was published in the afternoon. Those who won more than once gained enough prestige to be paid for their advice. "Smorfia" or dream books gained wide acceptance as guides. The story is told of the poor peasant who carried his winnings home in a wheelbarrow. A short time later he was offering some household articles for sale to get some money to play again. In America the lottery is conducted by "companies", who receive the numbers by wire from Italy every Saturday. These "companies" form a close group, barring others from entering the field.

The game of "bocce" is a great favorite with the men. The ball may be thrown as well as rolled, but the method is agreed upon beforehand. In Italy the game may be played on rough ground, while in Newark it is played on a regulation alley. This has taken some of the skill out of the game. Two or more players throw or roll a ball, each trying to see how close he can place his "pallo", large ball, to the "pallino", a smaller ball. The player whose ball comes closest to the "pallino" scores a point and throws the "pallino" for the next play. This continues until the team or individual scores 21 points.

Italians found children playing the same games as they played in the home country under different names. "La Spia" became "I Spy". "A Cavallo" was leap frog. Other childrens' games and field sports are common to both countries.

When the Italians migrated to Newark, their recreation was trans-

[3]Used in this country as roughly equivalent to cents.

ferred from the open air to indoors. With the exception of the Italian
Catholic Union, the Italians do not have a large hall in Newark in which
to hold their indoor activities.

MUSIC

Music occupies a conspicuous place in the life of the first generation Italians. They are firmly convinced that Italian music is the
world's greatest. Italian operas are always well attended. The
gallery of the Metropolitan Opera House in New York sees many Newark
Italians when one of the Italian operas is being performed. The folk
songs, however, are the prime favorites. The holiday seasons find
families joining in singing Neapolitan or other folk airs to the accompaniment of mandolin or guitar. No wedding, christening or similar
occasion is celebrated without this folk music. Some of the older
folks know dozens of these airs and are frequently called upon for
renditions. Outings are incomplete without spontaneous outpouring of
song.

The two outstanding types of folk songs are the Neapolitan Songs
and the Stornelli Romani. The former are presented to the public at a
annual festival in the Piedigrotta in Naples. The words and music are
romantically sentimental.

The words of the Stornelli, which has a contant tune, are made
up by two singers as they go along. The song frequently takes on an
insulting character which even leads to physical violence only averted
by the audience. Most of this, however, seems to be traditional and
in fun.

The radio has spread these songs and kept the Italian population in New Jersey informed on the latest ones.

Through the efforts of the Dante Alignieri Society, music lovers
have been entertained for years by some outstanding artists. The feature
of all Dante meetings is the social hour that closes them, making it
possible for people to get acquainted. At the end of the musical programs
the audience is invited to partake of a buffet.

The largest section of Newark's second generation Italians are also
music lovers, but of the jazz variety. A case of note is that of a
local stone-cutter who has accumulated some 5,000 records of every type
of music except jazz. His children think he should have made better
use of the money.

DANCES

The Italian folk dances, like their songs, are the simple form of
expressing their sorrows, joys, hopes and ambitions. Many are known to
have existed before Christianity. Because these dances of a simple
people have a national significance, feast days and national holidays
are incomplete without them.

Folk dances are participated in by one, two or more people. The
most popular are the Tarantella, the Furlana, of Venice, the Mazzucca[4]
La Ruggiera and La Siciliana. All of these dances are performed to
the accompaniment of the mandolin, guitar and tambourine.

The world at large accepts the Tarantella as Italy's national dance.
The young people think of it first because it is breezy and animated.
Its name is derived from the giant spider, the tarentola, whose bite

[4] Adopted from the Polish Masurka by early Italian immigrants.

produces an uncontrolled desire to dance. It was supposed that by
dancing to the point of exhaustion the dancer would be cured of the
insect's poison.

The second generation yields the floor to their elders when the
Italian orchestra starts an Italian dance. The second generation knows
little of these dances and seems to care less. Social dancing in
Newark draws a large following from among Italian youth. While the
parents try to restrict the activities of their daughters, there is more
freedom from their parents than their mothers had in Italy. At one
time the restrictions were enforced by a stern father, who would only
allow his daughter to dance at the annual affair held by his <u>societa</u>.
Today the youth choose one of the dancing halls and attend regularly
on Saturday night, without regard to which of the many "social" or
"athletic" clubs is sponsoring the affair.

THEATER

In Italy the theater had a regular place in the life of the city
population, while the towns waited for the appearance of a stock company.
The <u>Avellino Theater</u> for example, could expect with regularity the
arrival of such a company at Christmas time to give about ten performances
in the two-month schedule. The puppeteer with his marionette theater
was often a part of the entertainment on holidays.

The Newark Opera House is one of the few theaters that produce
Italian entertainment. Mr. Alfredo Carrigane, the director, is receiving
the support of the Italian community because he understands their
requirements.

The season lasts from Spetember first to May. Opera, drama, and

comedy are offered. In addition there are a number of Italian moving
pictures secured from the Esperia Film Company of New York. One of the
most famous of the Italian stereotype characters, Farfariello, has for
years been entertaining the Italian colonies with his imitations of
the various types of Italians in this country. In the moving pictures
the most popular male lead is Vittorio De Sica.

In many cases the dramatic company is already known through the
radio.

RADIO

The radio plays an important part in Italian recreation. It came
to the rescue of many illiterates and certainly improved their knowledge
of current events. Limited literacy and the continuous exigencies of the
struggle for existence have forced them to concentrate almost solely on
their jobs. The radio has brought recreation into the home and enlarged
their vision.

Five minor stations in the metropolitan area broadcast Italian
programs. Sponsors are usually of Italian extraction. Recently some
of the major stations (through the sponsorship of large advertisers)
have also been broadcasting in Italian. There are six major dramatic
companies playing in the Italian language. The dramas are run serially
but are repeated in full at the several local playhouses in the metropolitan area. The most popular of these plays are "The Neapolitan
Revolution", "Love of a Mother" and "The Miracles of the Madonna."

During the day the housewives' work is made easier by listening

to a dramatic play or humorous sketch.[5] In the evening the programs vary
from popular Italian folk songs to grand opera recordings.

Leading local Italian artists such as Laura Triggini, Mario Palerno,
Angelo Pilotto, Luigi Dalle Molle, Mario Le Dano, Filippa Anfuso, and
Teresa Genovese are presented from time to time. In addition authorities in the fields of Italian music, painting and literature address the
group. Important recitals are usually given in the Griffith auditorium
in Newark while other recitals are presented in the house of members.

OUTINGS

The picnic in all probability is a carryover from the Italian feast,
which in many instances was held in the country. In this country, the
strong influence of the second generation is easily detected at the
picnic. The music is for the most part of the jazz variety. When Italian
music is played some of the old folks make a brave attempt at folk
dancing. The majority of those attending still enjoy Italian food and
wine although the young and some of the old people can be seen eating
hot dogs and drinking beer or soda.

The same trend is followed in games, "Morra" and "Bocce" are
played by all, but baseball, handball, quoits and poker are played by
the younger generation. Most outings are run "stag". On the other
hand there are many women's organizations that conduct similar affairs
for women only.

Throughout the summer seashore outings to Long Branch are enjoyed

[5]The cultural level of the plays on the legitimate stage, in the movies
and on the radio are on a low level of mawkish sentimentality.

by Newark Italians of all generations. These differ from other affairs in that all members of the family go together. There is some patronage of other resorts, but Long Branch is still the most popular with New Jersey Italians.

NATIONAL HOLIDAYS

Italian national holidays, celebrated with much color, ceremony and enthusiasm are observed by both first and second generation Italians in Newark, although more of the first generation keep up the tradition. Those from Southern and Central Italy, of both generations, are more apt to observe their national holidays than their compatriots from the North and Sicily. The survey revealed that thirty per cent of first generation Italians, and twenty-four per cent of the second generation celebrated these occasions.

In commemoration of the granting of the Italian constitution on March 4, 1848, a celebration is held on the first Sunday in June.[6] Throughout Italy, April 21st is a day of festivities, for it is the birthday of ancient Rome.[7] The birthday of the king is observed by his subjects. One of the recent holidays is the anniversary of Italy's entry into the World War on May 24, 1915.[8] These are not widely celebrated in Newark.

[6]Pre-fascist.

[7]A part of the Fascist attempt to revive the glories of ancient Rome.

[8]This holiday was deemphasized with the growth of the Axis.

The most celebrated holiday is Columbus Day, October 12, which has been a national holiday in Italy since 1926. Newark celebrates the day at the Columbus Monument, in the center of the Broad Street side of Washington Park. Each year Italian civic, patriotic and religious groups sponsor the meeting which celebrates the memory and genius of Columbus. They spare no effort to make the occasion colorful and impressive. New Jersey is one of thirty-five states in which Columbus Day is a State Holiday.

CHAPTER XII

EDUCATION

Coming from a background of little or no educational advantages, and a rather rigid class system, the Italians, particularly from south Italy, had to develop desires for education. To date they have been one of the slowest of the immigrant groups to take advantage of American education. Italians, coming from a country where children were often expected to work even before they had reached their teens, could not understand compulsory education which forced a child to remain in school until well into his teens. The second generation inherited this attitude. Furthermore, their homes had no books, few newspapers, and no tradition of learning, no incentive to obtain more than the barest essentials of education.[1]

In 1911, according to Marsulli, there were more than 6,000 Italians in the school system. The Seventh Avenue school had 1,200 of them, while others such as the Franklin, 13th Avenue, Bergen Street, Burnett Street, Chestnut Street, Hamburg Place, Lafayette Street, Newton Street, North 7th Street and Webster Street had considerable numbers. He observed that most of these never reached high school,

---

[1] See Grace Irwin, "Michelangelo in Newark" (Harpers Monthly, v.143, p. 446-54. September, 1921) for an amusing and informative account of the difficulties of teaching art to young Italian immigrants.

either through lack of appreciation of the benefits of schooling or a desire to add children's earnings to the family budget. Marzulli was so impressed with the benefits of education that he exclaimed that the children would be better off if they could sleep in school. It was at this time that the present leaders of the colony were getting started, those who had the good judgment to see the benefits of higher education.

Much of the Italians withdrawal of children from school is conditioned by dire necessity. Nevertheless, bit by bit there has been an increasing participation in educational advantages as well as a change in attitude toward the school.

A profound respect for the professional man is part of the current attitude. About 40 per cent want their boys to become professionals.* About one-fourth of the first generation want their boys to become skilled workmen, but less than ten per cent of the second generation feel so. There is twice as much desire among the second generation parents to allow the boy to pick his own work as among the first generation. Other ambitions are scattered. Italians, from all parts of Italy, have an equal respect for the professions. Over half of the first generation parents want their daughters to be either professionals or white collar workers, and a similar trend is noticeable in the second generation. There is a drop from 25 per cent to less than ten per cent from one generation to the other in the desire that daughters should merely learn to be good housewives. Again all groups of Italians agree.

So persistent has been the American emphasis on education that 84 per cent of the first generation and 83 per cent of the second replied

*Data drawn from the general questionnaire.

in the affirmative when asked if good schooling helps to get good jobs for their children. There was, however, somewhat more doubt expressed in the remainder of the second generation than of the first as to education helping at all. However, while 11 percent answered that they did not know in the first generation, this fell to only 3 per cent in the second.

When questioned as to the amount of schooling necessary to get a good job, about 10 per cent of both groups thought grammar school or trade school enough, while an additional 50 per cent thought high school sufficient. The remaining 40 per cent thought college would be needed. Less than 1 per cent declared that schooling was not necessary.

Preference for the public school as against the parochial school showed some increase in the second generation. Fifty-three per cent of the first and 60 per cent of the second generation preferred public schools. However, one-third of the first generation and one-fifth of the second admitted that they did not know which was best. In Newark, in 1940, there were about 2,700 Italian children in parochial schools of a total enrollment of 12,000, or 22 per cent.

Of the 27 parochial schools there are only three in which no Italians are found. These are Polish. Students in those attached to Italian churches such as St. Philip Neri, St. Francis Xavier, St. Lucy's and Our Lady of Mt. Carmel are practically all Italian. Others range from 58 per cent Italian in Sacred Heart to 2.6 per cent at St. Benedict's.

The Italians in Newark today express little preference, as compared with the other children, for schooling of the oldest son or daughter.

Less than ten per cent thought it important that either the oldest son
or daughter should have better schooling. On the contrary they were
more inclined to the idea that the oldest child start to work early in
order that the younger children may be better taken care of. It is
common to hear of second or third children getting their education
through the oldest child's efforts.

The oldest children of about 30 per cent of the first generation
people have little or no schooling, having passed the school age before
they reached America. Of those who have schooling, about two-thirds had
not gotten further than grammer school in 1939. Of the balance, only
4 per cent had had any college training. However, about 40 per cent of
the oldest children of first generation people are still in school, so
that eventually there may be a somewhat higher educational level. It
is significant, however, that education is only slightly better in the
second generation. But two-thirds of the second generation oldest
children are still in school, and the gap in training between the
two generations will undoubtedly increase.

In a survey conducted by the Newark Board of Education in 1936,
it was found that there were 14,156 children with parents born in Italy,
or 32 per cent of the white elementary school population. Probably the
next highest percentage is Jewish. The survey did not distinguish
between Polish Jews and Poles or Russian Jews and Russians. The total
Russian second generation was 14.9 per cent of 3,903 and the Polish
9 per cent of 2,350. Twelve of the 53 elementary schools have over
75 per cent of their second generation population Italian and 24 have
more than 50 per cent.

The Rotary Club of Newark made two surveys of nationality in Newark Schools. The first in 1923 showed 1,613 pupils born in Italy and 19,817 with fathers born in Italy. In the high schools, Barringer had 23.5% of its population with fathers born in Italy, Central 11.0% and East Side 14.8%. In the elementary schools those with Italian fathers amounted to 29% as compared with 28.5% of native white parentage and 42.5% in all the other categories. A recheck in 1927 showed the Italian parentage in elementary school had risen to 30.4%.

Of the six high schools in 1942, three had substantial Italian population. Barringer High School, with a total enrollment of 1,751, had about 55% Italian-origin registration. In the first year about 75% were Italian in origin; the percentages thin out in the second, third and fourth years. Of the January, 1942, graduating class's highest ten students seven were of Italian extraction. As far back as 1898 there were no Italians in the school but they are steadily moving into the neighborhood. There are at present 328 students taking Italian.

In Central High School there is a total enrollment of 2,805 of which 55% are Italian. 150 of these are studying Italian. Here of the 25 top graduates in 1942, 5 were Italian girls.

East Side High School's enrollment is 2,464. 25 to 30 per cent of these are Italian of which 91 are studying Italian. 6 Italians were found in the top thirty graduated in January, 1942.

West Side High School, the only other with a substantial Italian enrollment, has 2,589 students, one-third of whom are Italian. 230 of these study Italian. They maintain the relative percentage of those graduating with honors.

In 1910 there were no more than two score Italian students in the high schools.[2] The growth in high school attendance is enormous.

The general conclusion of these figures is obvious. The teaching problem in Newark is largely one of adapting children of immigrants into the general community. It is, therefore, imperative that the school system have a full understanding of the problem involved in teaching these children of two cultures.

The present case of nerves which the Italians of Newark are suffering due to the war as well as the fear of college administration of hurting their feelings is well exemplified by the Newark College of Engineering which refused to give figures of Italian enrollment. Their refusal was in the following terms:

"We have discussed the matter with members of our student body and faculty who are of Italian extraction and after giving the matter thorough consideration, we feel that we must again refuse to make the information available at this time. The men with whom we talked tell us that their parents and relatives are bewildered and disturbed by the finger printing and registering of aliens which is necessary in many cases. Many of them do not understand the purpose of the registration and are afraid of what may result from the information now being collected."

The enrollment of the University of Newark is given below. The

_____

[2]Information obtained from William Melivitsky, supervisor of foreign languages in the Newark Public Schools.

interesting fact revealed here is the small percentage of Italians
receiving higher education in either liberal arts or the professions.
Also significant is the large amount of intermarriage revealed here in
the difference between those with both parents Italian and those with
only one parent Italian. It is much more than the general population

ITALIAN NATIONALITY BACKGROUND
Of The
STUDENTS OF THE UNIVERSITY OF NEWARK

(As of November 1, 1941)

SCHOOL	BOTH PARENTS ITALIAN	ONE PARENT ITALIAN	ENROLLMENT
School of Business	25	14	472
College of Arts & Science	22	2	236
Law School	7	-	125
TOTAL	54	16	833

The Newark State Teachers College has a total enrollment of 484.
Classification of national origin was done by names and so is open to
criticism, out the figures indicate that 57 of these are Italian or
about 11.7%. This average holds constant throughout the years with
10% of Seniors, 12.5% of Juniors, 11.5% of Sophmores and 12.5% of Freshmen.
The population of Newark, it must be remembered, is about 20% Italian or
Italian in origin. This enrollment shows the tremendous strides which
the Italians have made in technical educational advances and also reveals
how far they have to go.

CHAPTER XIII

ITALIAN PUBLIC OPINION

Italian public opinion is the result of various influences which have been at work on the Italian communities since their inception. Although there are of course differences of individual opinion, the colonies tend to all into certain rather well defined patterns. As is usual in any group, informal word of mouth communications are a most potent factor in creating general attitudes. These, of course, are difficult to measure objectively.

Investigations were made as to the attitude of Newark Italians toward the more formal influences such as the radio and newspapers. There are in general two types of radio programs and newspapers with influence among these people, those in Italian or about Italians and those which are American in language and general interest. The foreign press and radio are again of two kinds, those originating here and those originating abroad. With these formal and informal influences as a background, an attempt was made to measure attitudes toward other ethnic groups.

Among the most striking informal influences are those which preserve interest in Italy and things Italian. This interest is preserved both by natural inclination and as a defense against the unreceptive American community. In the first generation, where the use of English is faulty or nonexistent, opinions derive almost exclusively from the

Italian colony and its institutions. Mussolini's adventures and progress
are thoroughly discussed in the little town (paesani),clubs (circoli).
In relations between Italy and the United States as symbols, the
United States would be favored. But on specific issues with specific
personalities involved there is apt to be criticism of American officials.
President Roosevelt's "knife in the back" speech was severely criticized
as being unfair, although Roosevelt until that time had been extremely
popular. Furthermore, many italians who went all the way with
Roosevelt in his condemnation of Mussolini balked at this particular
phrase.

The general feeling toward Italy before the war was admiration of
Mussolini's successes in world affairs and the efficiency of the fascist
regime. Most impressive to the Italians is the success of the corpor-
ative state in doing away with unemployment and the public works
program. Mussolini was decidedly less popular among the north Italians
than among their southern brethern. One large club of the former bans
his picture from their club rooms. Even this reflects the situation in
Italy.

Much of the discussion, however, centers around community personalities and incidents. Italians of the first generation have a tremendous
loyalty to people who do them favors. To control their vote it is
merely necessary to have one person in each club who can do favors.
There is no political philosophy involved at all. These Italians from
the days of the padrone have been accustomed to look to some individual
for advice and help. Always there have been those who have been willing
to assume this role. In politics, especially, the result has been full

participation in and acceptance of the patronage system. Certain key
men in the colony thus lead Italian political opinion among the first
generation.

As a result of their European and American experience first generation Italians expect hard manual labor as part of the normal scheme of
things. Their attitude toward work is therefore serious and consci-
entious. On the other hand a source of continual strife is the second
generation's more American and more casual attitude. Instead of an end
in existence, work is decidedly a means to the young Italian. Even
more than the average adolescent he dreams continuously of becoming a
politician, a figure in the sports world, a chicken farmer or in some
way rising by a not too difficult path to a social and economic level
above his parents. Parents are apt to disapprove.

The family is the center of existence for the Italian born.
Children are expected to be obedient, respectful and hard working. Boys
are given some leeway in their sex life, but girls must be as blameless
as Caesar's wife. Wives are expected to concern themselves with the
home and children. Although there has been a decrease of restrictions
affecting the social relationship between the sexes, there is still
considerable parental restraint. Those who violate the strictness of
the code must suffer the father's discipline, exercised with hand or
tongue.

The second generation is considerably freer and more under the
American influence in its attitude toward the relative position of the
sexes. There are, however, considerable numbers of second generation
girls who have accepted the patriarchial family and fit into the home

as wife and mother in much the same manner as their mothers did.

The relative trust in radio and newspaper as a source of news seems to be about even among those of the first generation questioned in Newark. Considerable numbers said they trusted neither.[1]

The second generation, on the other hand, showed slightly more trust in radio news. The growing reliance of all low-income groups on the radio at the expense of the newspaper is a countrywide phenomenon. The first generation distrust of either source was cut to about half in the second generation. This picture holds true particularly for southern Italians and Sicilians. But the central and northern Italians have less tendency to trust radio news over newspapers in the second generation. This phenomenon is probably due to a superior educational background, as this generally has been found to be a factor n choice of newspapers over radio.

Distrust of both radio and newspapers seems to decline as the Italians get away from the old country traditions. Of those who trust neither source of information over two-thirds have made a serious effort to inculcate old country traditions in their children.

In the first generation the unskilled laborer and the housewife trust radio as a source of news, while the skilled laborer prefers newspapers. In all other occupations there is no distinction except that among the first generation a majority of those who own their own businesses prefer newspapers.

Except among the skilled workers, the second generation trusts radio news more than newspapers. Skilled workers indicate little choice.

[1]See Appendix I for tabulations.

This preference for radio is particularly true of the Sicilians where even in the skilled category the radio is trusted more.

There is nothing unusual about the relative trust placed by the Italians in radio and newspapers; they are a part of general American trends.

First generation Italians are bound strongly to the foreign language paper. Some few read newspapers printed in Italy, but the Italian-American papers interest them more. However, about half of the first generation who made a choice read American newspapers most. One fifth of the first generation read no newspaper at all probably because of inability to read.

Many Italians who answered which newspaper they read most were unwilling to answer which they trust most. Among those answering, there was a decided drop in trust in the Italian paper published both here and abroad. Those who refused to answer were largely south Italians and Sicilians. Those who read American newspapers most seemed also to trust them most.

Of those in the first generation who prefer English language radio programs 85 per cent also prefer American newspapers and only 9.5 per cent prefer Italian-American papers. Radio programs in Italian survive better in the second generation than the newspapers do, primarily because the second generation has only a speaking knowledge of the language.

Of the specific newspapers read, Generoso Pope's Il Progresso Italo-Americano (The Italian-American Progressive) is unquestionably the leader among the first generation. Of the Italian papers, Pope's

Il Corriere D'America is next. Both follow identical editorial policies.
Il Progresso offers its readers, besides general news f the world, such
features as news of the individual regions of Italy and a page devoted
to Italian activities in New Jersey. Editorially Il Progresso has
given a sympathetic interpretation of Mussolini's Italy, and better
Italian-American understanding is one of its announced policies.[2] The
largest selling English language paper is the Newark News, the leading
local newspaper. The News is conservative, nominally independent
Democrat. The more sophisticated members of the community read the
New York papers and take the local newspaper for its local items. The
local Italian press serves the same purpose for news of the Italian
community. Generally speaking the second generation reads the same
newspapers as the general community, with more interest in the
tabloids than the first generation.

The radio has penetrated the home life of Italians just as much
as that of their fellow Americans. The Italian better than any other
group is served by a station which can satisfy all of his needs. This
station, WOV, in New York, has complete coverage of music, plays, news
and special features, all concentrating on Italian interests. Italian
business men buy time on the air to advertise their products. Slightly
less than half the first generation indicated that it was their
favorite station. Of the four small stations which have Italian programs, WBNX AND WHOM are the most popular. One tenth of the American
born Italians express preference for them. Otherwise most of the

---

[2] "Il Progresso" shifted its focus of attention when it saw the hand-
writing on the wall of the impending war. It is now quite blatantly
anti-Mussolini.

Italians prefer WABC of the Columbia Broadcasting System. The preference for WOV is particularly strong among south Italians and Sicilians.[3]

Overwhelmingly the Italians do listen to Italian programs even if they are not favorites, and only 13 per cent of the first generation never listen to Italian programs. The proportion falls to one-half in the second generation. Of the first generation listeners, over half are steady devotees of Italian programs, while less than a quarter of the second generation listeners do it consistently. Asked which kind they preferred, English or Italian programs, even some of those who listen only occasionally to Italian programs claimed that they preferred them. There were also many who expressed no preference. No significant difference was found among Italians from different sections of Italy.

There was essentially no difference in listening to Italian programs for those on relief to those earning over $3,000 a year except in the second generation, where it was found that the more money was earned the less listening there was to Italian programs.

Slightly over a quarter of the first generation interviewed had short wave radio sets. The proportion owning them increased with income, the normal condition in the population at large.[4]

Magazine reading among first generation Italians is very slight. Almost none read magazines published in Italy, while very few read Italian-American magazines. Such Italian magazines as exist have a limited circulation and are not a factor in Italian thinking. Almost

[3] Figures compiled in 1939.

[4] See Appendix I for tabulations of various aspects of reading and listening habits of Italians, Germans, Jews and Poles.

two-thirds of the first generation do not read any kind of magazines. One-sixth read American magazines. The second generation Italian reads American magazines if any. Almost half, however, read no magazines at all. Sicilians and south Italians are particularly uninterested. Such magazines as are read are those of the type of Life, Liberty and the Saturday Evening Post.

Both groups vote overwhelmingly for the greater trustworthiness of American magazines. Most, however, refused to answer this question. This refusal extended to Italians from all sections of Italy.

What has resulted from the contacts of the Italian with the press, radio, magazines and other immeasurable contacts from the world about them? Among the most interesting effects are the attitudes toward other groups in the population. In general these attitudes reflect the feelings of the community. The sole exception is of course their attitudes toward other Italians. However, as has been pointed out before, there do exist prejudices among Italians toward people from other sections of Italy than themselves.

Three hundred and fifty first generation and 244 second generation Italians were asked their attitudes toward other nationalities and races on seven points: tolerance toward entry of these groups into the United States, toward their becoming citizens, living in the same neighborhood, working at the same job, belonging to the same organization, coming to their homes as guests and intermarrying with them.

They were questioned about the British, Negroes, Irish, Scandinavians, Jews, Italians, Orientals, Poles, Germans, Russians, Hungarians and a nonexistent group, Pireneans. This last was included to discover whether Italians reacted against unfamiliar names, as well as ones they could possibly have known.

The greatest antipathies in all questions among first generation respondents were toward Orientals and Negroes. Strangely enough, there was little objection to their entering the country or becoming citizens. Beyond that the Italians wanted nothing to do with them. The other groups were much less frowned upon. About one-half, however, displayed antipathy toward the Jews on one question or another. This was particularly true in their desire to exclude them from their families and their organizations. There is less feeling, but it is still substantial, against Russians. Next in order come the Scandinavians, Irish, Poles and Pireneans. The high position of the Pireneans, considering the fact that 68 Italians recognized that there was no such thing, signifies that prejudices tend to be unfounded. This is by no means confined to Italians but is true of the general population. There is less antagonism to the British and Germans than to any of the other groups. Anti-British feeling is relatively new in Italy, as is pro-German feeling. Thus the first generation still shares exactly the feelings of the general community.

The second generation displays more tolerance. Nevertheless, prejudices against Negroes, Orientals and Jews were the more pronounced. The British, Germans and Irish were in high favor. Objections to intermarriage ranked highest, but here was also much opposition to being in the same neighborhood and joining the same organizations as the other groups.

A considerably larger number were cognizant of the non-existence

of Pireneans. The indications of the survey are that the second generation is more tolerant than the first and displays more rationality in
its judgments. There are indications that more contacts between groups
breed more tolerance. Compared to the other nationalities studied,
the Italians displayed one of the best tolerance scores. On the whole
their prejudices as between the various nationality groups reflect the
attitudes of the general community.

[5]See Bogardus, op. cit., p. 25.

CHAPTER XIV

PRESENT ADJUSTMENT

The Italians are at present in a highly amorphous state. In the
various fields of human activity it is impossible to confine them
in toto to any one attern. The historical development of the various
Italian institutions snows how multitypical they are. One writer on
the Italians has divided them economically into the tenement type, the
trade or business type, the professional type, and the Y.CA and college
type.[1] But it is more than that. There is the division into regional
types dependent on geographical origins. Above all, there is the
ever-widening schism between the first and second generations. However, in Newark there is a cultural continuity from the old country
and an, at times tenuous but real, in-group feeling based on the
concept "Italian". It may range from a vague fellow-feeling at the
casual introduction of two Italian coll ge graduates to the purposeful
Italianism of the Italian politician. The concept Italian, too, will
mean different things to different Italians, and by no means has the
same connotation as it did in Italy. Generalizations, then, are not
applicable to all Italians and are only as true as most generalizations.
With this warning in mind the more common attitudes and behavior patterns

[1]Mariano, op. cit., Chap. VIII

may be summarized.

The first and second generations are participants in the community at large principally through their economic activities. For the older people this is essentially a masculine participation, while the young includes a large number of girls. The mores of Italy which looked to training for home and motherhood for girls has yielded to the call of the American factory and, to a lesser extent, of offices and the professions. The participation of the foreign-born is limited, however, by the fact that the small shopkeeper is usually servicing an Italian population with Italian products. For shoemakers and barbers this is less true. Professional men are more likely to have Italian clients in both generations. A broadening influence is the work of the trade unions which are attempting to replace the national in-groups of the city with economic in-groups.

In the family the closeness of the first generation group is still typical and a great sense of the interresponsibility of the greater family is prevalent. Intermarriage is breaking down the barriers in the second generation, but very slowly, inasmuch as most of the opportunities are in the Italian framework and as there is a great prejudice against the practice by the old people. The everyday functioning of the family group is patriarchal in control, with the customary more subtle female controls also present. Children are struggling against this and creating the conflict situations between generations and cultures. Food habits are Italian with infiltration of American foods. The second generation is similar, but less rigid and more touched by American standards, symbolized by their use of English almost exclusively.

The Roman Catholic Church is still the focus of religious life for both generations. The original segregation impulse is still strong, especially in the first generation. The Italian Catholic churches are still staffed with foreign-born and foreign-trained priests, who have little influence on the larger affairs of the diocese where the Irish and, to a lesser degree, the Germans are in control. The old people are regular attendants at the Italian churches and the second generation, particularly the girls, are quite religious. There is a certain amount of attendance at other Catholic churches which is a function of the economic standing of the Italian. That is, those with more money in either generation may live in a non-Italian neighborho d and attend a non-Italian church. The second generation, with some exceptions, has a much more casual attitude toward the Church.

The political life of the Italian is bound up with their in-group feeling again. They are extremely conscious of the prestige and power inherent in public office. In both parties, however, they participate as Italians in connection with the Italian vote. Various social clubs, for example, are convertible into political clubs at the proper time. The changing international situation has brought them to disapprove of Mussolini, whose influence in world affairs had given him enormous prestige. The Italian Consul, prior to his ejection from Newark, had been an honored guest and a powerful propagandist in the various organizations. Now they feel that Mussolini has been stupid or has double-crossed them.

Still rankling is the dislike for England, dating from the application of sanctions to Italy, although the position of England as an ally has made this position less and less tenable. They fully realize the dilemma.

Their organizational life is largely Italian centered. Here, however, the centering is Italian-American rather than Italian. This is true of most of the American activities of the Italians and has been true except in discussing international affairs. Organizations which at one time either consciously or unconsciously disseminated Fascist propaganda are now bewildered by the turn of events. It must be remembered that America in general has only recently been uniform in its condemnation of Mussolini. The mutual aid features of the organizations are gradually yielding to American insurance companies and in this sense full participation in American life is a fixture of second generation families.

American recreation facilities (topped by the radio and the movies) have swept the second generation. The first generation is spotty in its movie attendance, but the old people are generally not movie-goers. The radio, however, attracts the first generation particularly to Italian programs ranging from music to soap operas. Considerable home entertaining is characteristic of both generations.

Education is ever more widespread as the power of educated man becomes more and more obvious. They still do not have their proper proportion in any of the high schools or colleges, but this is rapidly being changed. The schools, of course, are a notable example of enforced relationships with other groups and are a potent force in the breakdown of the intermarriage barriers.

The Italians of Newark, then, are still a readily distinguishable

group. Most of their joint activities are in terms of Italian-Americanism
rather than Italianism. With the gradual increase in the economic and
educational level as the generations succeed each other, the isolation
is breaking down and another two generations will probably see the
last of it. There seems to be little indication that the Italians will
succeed in maintaining their identity in later generations in the way
that the Irish have.

APPENDIX I

FOREIGN LANGUAGE BROADCASTS

and

NEWSPAPER READING

A comparative study was done in cooperation with the Princeton Radio Research Project, now the Office of Radio Research at Columbia University of foreign language broadcasts and newspaper reading. The Office of Radio Research helped formulate the questionnaire in return for having the following questions inserted about foreign language broadcasts and newspaper reading:

Do you listen to radio programs in the language of the old country from American stations: Often__Sometimes__Never__

Do you read newspapers in the language of the old country? 1/
_____

Do you prefer programs in the language of the old country or in English or in Jewish?

What newspapers do you read most? Old Country__ American__Old Country-American__Jewish__None__

What news broadcasts do you most trust? Old country__American__ Old Country-American__None__

Which newspapers do you most trust? Old Country__ American__Old Country-American__Jewish__None__

What is your favorite radio station?_____

In what newspaper do you find the most reliable news?_____2/

What news do you most trust? Radio__Newspaper__Neither__ Don't know__None__

_____

1/ This question was added late in the course of the field work. The sample obtained is therefore considerably smaller.

2/ Asked only of Newark respondents.

Do you have a shortwave set or
access to one?

If yes, do you listen to shortwave broadcasts from the old
country? Often__Sometimes__
Never__

If no, if you had one would you
listen to shortwave broadcasts
from the old country?__

Do you listen to Jewish programs?__

The objectives were to compare reading and radio habits
of immigrants, with stress on generation and nationality
differences. There is a considerable part of the public with
opinions on the desirability and effect of foreign language
newspapers and radio programs, but with little or no knowledge
of the actual situation. Tabulations on this study indicate
at least the attitudes of immigrants toward the relative values
of English and foreign language media of communication.

Who Was Interviewed

Included in this part of the study were first and second
generation Germans, Poles, Italians, and Russian Jews. Most
of them lived in Newark, New Jersey. Some of the questions
were asked of Italians living in Trenton, some of the Poles in
Paterson. The exact number of respondents in each group is
shown below, in Table 1.

Table 1

NATIONALITY OF FIRST AND SECOND GENERATION RESPONDENTS
by Residence

Nationality	Newark First Generation	Newark Second Generation	Trenton & Paterson First Generation	Trenton & Paterson Second Generation	All Residences First Generation	All Residences Second Generation
Poles	168	116	79	42	247	158
Italians	350	244	290	80	640	324
Russian Jews	228	227	--	--	228	227
Germans	87	133	--	--	87	133
All Nationalities	833	720	369	122	1202	842

For a description of respondents by age, income, education, and occupation, refer to Appendix II. For an account of how interviews were assigned, see Appendix III.

Short Wave Listening Habits

The most direct contact an immigrant group can have with the home country is by shortwave. One would expect first generation respondents, therefore, to listen to shortwave broadcasts more frequently than second generation respondents. And we find that among those Germans, Italians and Poles who have access to shortwave sets, [1] listening is almost twice as heavy in the first generation as in the second.

[1] Roughly one-third of the sample, excluding Jews, have access to shortwave sets. The Jews are not reported in this part of the study because there are no Hebrew or Yiddish shortwave stations in Europe and Russian shortwave is comparatively feeble. Excluding Jews, then, we find no significant difference in shortwave ownership either by generation or by nationality.

Table 2

LISTENING TO SHORTWAVE FROM THE OLD COUNTRY
By First and Second Generation Respondents.

Frequency of Listening	First Generation %	Second Generation %
Often	15	4
Sometimes	47	29
Never	38	67
Total	100	100

About 60 per cent of the first generation with access to shortwave sets listen often or sometimes to broadcasts from their old countries, but only about 30 per cent in the second generation with access to shortwave sets. Of all first generation immigrants about 19% listen to shortwave from the old country. In the second generation about 12% do. Shortwave listening then is related to psychological nearness to the old country.

Acknowledging this relation, we can then show in Table 3 [1]/ that the Poles with shortwave sets in the New Jersey area

1/ This table does not take account of the composition of the three nationalities by generation. There are more first than second generation respondents among the Poles, but more second generation among the Germans. It would be possible to give the results in a standardized form so as to assume the same proportion of first and second generation in all three nationality groups. In a number of tables, the computation shows, however, that the final results would be hardly changed because the variations are so small. Furthermore, the different composition as to generations is probably not a sampling error, but characteristic of the three different nationality groups in this area, so that they are better characterized by the straight adding of the first and second generations.

studied lose their attachment to the old country more slowly
than the Italians, and the Italians more slowly than the
Germans.

Table 3

LISTENING TO SHORTWAVE FROM THE OLD COUNTRY
by Nationality

Frequency of listening	Poles %	Italians %	Germans %
Often or sometimes	67	56	51
Never	33	44	49
Total	100	100	100

Other aspects of the study indicate the same order of
attachment.

Listening to Local Foreign Language Programs

Much more important than shortwave listening is the listening to foreign broadcasts coming from local American stations.
In the New York metropolitan area there are local stations --
WBNX, WHOM, WEVD, WAAT, WOV -- which spend a considerable part
of their time on foreign broadcasts in different languages.
The immigrants, therefore, have a chance to listen to programs
in the old idiom, to an extent which varies from group to group,
the amount of Italian broadcasts being much greater than that
of any other language group.

As a result, it was appropriate to ask the respondents
whether they listened to radio programs in the language of the
old country from American stations.

The following table shows that, at least in the first generation, this listening is considerable, and in the second generation it has not yet disappeared.

Table 4

FREQUENCY OF LISTENING TO LOCAL FOREIGN LANGUAGE BROADCASTS
by First and Second Generation Respondents

Frequency of Listening	First Generation %	Second Generation %
Often	37	10
Sometimes	36	30
Never	27	60
Total per cent	100	100

One-third of the first generation listens often, and over two-thirds at least sometimes to such programs. In the second generation, 40 per cent listen at least sometimes.

This attachment to the old country among first generation immigrants and the decreased attachment in the second generation are also reflected in the tabulation of types of stations preferred. The results of the tabulations are presented in Table 5.

Table 5

PREFERENCES AMONG THREE TYPES OF STATIONS
by First and Second Generation Respondents.

Type of Station Preferred	First Generation %	Second Generation %
Network	52	84
Local with foreign program	39	5
Other local	9	11
Total per cent	100	100

The mentioning of big network stations increases sharply from the first to the second generation, and the foreign language stations actually peter out. The small local stations, however, hold their own. We interpret this result as meaning that the second generation is Americanized as far as language goes, but the economic rise is not equally pronounced, and it therefore retains the interest in small stations which is characteristic of low income groups.

Again, national differences are observed when the first and second generation of each group are considered together, as in Table.6.

Table 6

PREFERENCE AMONG THREE TYPES OF STATIONS
by Nationality

Type of Station Preferred	Poles	Italians	Russian Jews	Germans
	%	%	%	%
Network	72	61	74	89
Local with foreign programs	21	32	19	6
Other local	7	7	7	5
Total per cent	100	100	100	100

With their negligible mentions of local stations with foreign programs and their frequent mentions of network stations, the Germans seem to be the most Americanized. Next in order of Americanization are the Russian Jews [1]; last are the Poles and Italians. That the Italians show greater preference for foreign language stations than the Poles is largely due to Station WOV, which specializes in Italian programs.

Although almost three-quarters of the first generation listen to some foreign language broadcasts, only 56% per cent trust the foreign news programs more than the American. Ease of understanding, and old associations, not trust, therefore, play the most important role in determining listening to local foreign language broadcasts.

[1] Whenever reference is made to Jewish foreign language reading and listening, both Russian and Yiddish are meant.

Reading Foreign Language Newspapers

The reading of foreign language newspapers is another measure of attachment to the old country culture. Whereas 75 per cent of the first generation read foreign language newspapers, 1/ only 34 per cent of the second generation do.

Table 7

READING NEWSPAPERS IN THE LANGUAGE OF OLD COUNTRY
by First and Second Generation Respondents

Frequency of Reading	First Generation %	Second Generation %
Often	42	17
Sometimes	34	17
Never	24	66
Total per cent	100	100

Credence in the foreign language press drops much more markedly than reading among second generation respondents. As can be seen from Table 8, only an insignificant fraction of the second generation believes in the reliability of the foreign press.

Furthermore, the longer first generation immigrants have been in the country, the less they trust the foreign language papers. An additional tabulation showed that of those who

1/ Most of these are foreign language papers published locally, but some are Old Country papers.

trust foreign papers most, only 11 per cent had been in the
United States before 1900, while of those who trust American
papers most, 33 per cent had been here since before 1900.

Table 8

PAPER IN WHICH MOST RELIABLE NEWS FOUND*
by First and Second Generation Respondents.

Type of Newspaper	First Generation %	Second Generation %
Metropolitan	13	30
Foreign	44	02
Local	43	68
Total per cent	100	100

*This is a question referring to a specific paper.
When asked as a check what type of newspaper was
trusted most, foreign or American, the results
were substantially the same.

The metropolitan dailies gain a larger percentage of
second generation trust than do the local papers. This points
to the increasing sophistication of the American born.

By nationality, reported in Table 9, considerable differences are again found. Trust in the foreign press is low
among the Germans. Such trust is held, however, by about one-
third of the Poles and ranges down to about one-fourth of
the Jews.

Table 9

PAPER IN WHICH MOST RELIABLE NEWS FOUND
by Nationality

Type of Newspaper	Poles %	Italians %	Russian Jews %	Germans %
Metropolitan	24	12	37	11
Foreign	32	26	23	6
Local	44	62	40	83
Total per cent	100	100	100	100

The Germans are probably local newspaper readers because they are better established and more settled, and thus community conscious. The Jews, on the other hand, are a better educated and more sophisticated group and would be attracted by the New York papers.

The percentage of immigrants reading foreign newspapers is much greater than the percentage who trust the news in them. It may be assumed, therefore, that they are read for news of the homeland, because of lack of familiarity with English, and for the general associations involved.

And it should be noted that of 452 foreign language newspaper readers, fully 57 per cent read the American newspapers more. As one can see in Table 10, this 57 per cent is an over-all picture for the four nationalities. When each group is considered separately, there is a 45 per cent variation, with the Poles again showing the strongest link

to the old country culture and the Germans showing the
weakest link. 1/

Table 10

PERCENT OF FOREIGN PAPER READERS
WHO READ AMERICAN PAPERS
THE MOST

Favored Paper	Poles	Italians	Jews	Germans	All Nationalities
Read American papers most	39	61	74	84	57
Total Per Cent) reading foreign papers)	100	100	100	100	100

Radio-Newspaper Comparison

Both newspaper and radio habits are indices of adherence
to an old country culture. But which index reflects the
adherence more finely? A tentative answer can be found by
comparing the drop from first to second generation in foreign
language reading with the drop in listening. From Table 7,
one calculates a 42 per cent drop in reading, from Table 4, a
33 per cent drop in listening. This indicates that the
reading of foreign language newspapers does not survive as
much as the listening to foreign language broadcasts.

Both reading of foreign language newspapers and listening
to foreign language programs drop with increasing income. For

---

1/ In the newspaper field the supply in each foreign language
is not so different as to obscure the greater assimilation
of the Italians when compared with the Poles. This greater
assimilation is obscured in the radio field because of the
strong Italian station, WOV.

listening, this is not startling, because it is known from
other studies that people in the higher economic brackets
generally listen less to the radio. 1/ The drop is merely
sharper than would ordinarily be expected within the neces-
sarily narrow range of incomes covered in a study of
immigrants. The drop in reading, however, is really striking..
Ordinarily, the trend is reversed. As income increases, people
are usually more likely to read newspapers. Increasing income
for immigrants, however, increases their opportunities for
Americanization. Consequently, fewer read Old Country-
American newspapers. Table 11 cites the per cent at each of
three income levels who never hear foreign language programs
and the per cent at each of three income levels who never read
foreign language papers. Only the first generation is reported.

Table 11

PER CENT AT EACH INCOME LEVEL
WHO NEVER HEAR FOREIGN LANGUAGE BROADCASTS
AND WHO NEVER READ FOREIGN LANGUAGE NEWSPAPERS

Income	Never Hear Foreign Language Broadcasts %	Never Read Foreign Language Newspapers %
Below $1,000	26	24
$1,000 up to $2,000	40	19
$2,000 and over	58	42

1/ See Lazarsfeld, Paul F., Radio and the Printed Page, Duell,
Sloan and Pearce, 1940.

Whatever the income there is a high correlation between radio and newspaper preferences among first generation respondents. 1/ One can find this by cross-tabulating replies to almost any questions about newspapers with any of the questions about radio. In one analysis, type of newspaper most trusted was cross-tabulated with the language preferred on radio programs. The results are reported in Table 12.

Table 12

NEWSPAPERS TRUSTED BY PROGRAMS PREFERRED
Among First Generation Respondents

| Programs Preferred | Newspapers Trusted | |
	Foreign Language	American
	No.	No.
Foreign Language	167	62
American	37	418
Total	204	480

Those who trust foreign newspapers prefer foreign programs; those who trust American newspapers prefer American programs.

The 23 persons who trust foreign language newspapers but prefer American programs are mostly Jewish. This phenomenon is probably due to the unsophisticated quality of Jewish programs as compared to the long established and first class Jewish newspapers. The 62 who trust American newspapers most

---

1/ There is not enough preference for foreign language communication in the second generation to warrant similar analysis.

but prefer foreign language programs are distributed among
the different nationalities in about the same proportion as
the general sample. However they are definitely an older
age group as 88 per cent are over forty. They thus have had
more opportunity to acquire reading skill in English.

In Table 13 still another cross-tabulation reveals the
interchangeability of the two indices. Papers voted for as
having the most reliable news were analyzed by type of local
radio station preferred.

Table 13

PAPERS WITH MOST RELIABLE NEWS BY FAVORITE STATIONS
Among First and Second Generation Respondents

Favorite Radio Station	Papers With Most Reliable News	
	Foreign Language	American
	No.	No.
Foreign Language	176	59
American	52	790
Total	228	849

The correlation between foreign language reading and
listening is again seen.

That foreign language listening habits are related to
foreign language reading and that both are stronger among
first generation families means that they are more important
for families who have stronger ties with the Old Country. By
this fact, however, such families tend to sustain the
psychological attachment. The practical conclusions would

depend upon one's general philosophy toward the immigration problem. One might welcome or deplore the whole foreign language broadcast and newspaper situation. Whatever his point of view, whoever wants to reach immigrants will find these media a powerful point of approach.

Another Index of Americanization

The attitude toward radio or newspapers is but one sign of a more generalized attitude toward the whole complex of the transmission from one culture to another. There are other signs which can be used. One is the teaching of Old Country traditions to the children in the family. [1] This index is positively correlated with the other two which have already been discussed. In Table 14, one can see that immigrants who keep the traditions of the old environment alive in their family are also likely to rely on news broadcasts in their native tongue over local stations.

Table 14

NEWS BROADCASTS MOST TRUSTED
BY TEACHING OF OLD COUNTRY TRADITIONS
Among First Generation Respondents

Teaches Old Country Traditions	News Broadcasts Most Trusted		
	Foreign Language	American	Total
	No.	No.	No.
Often or sometimes	155	91	246
Never	91	203	294
Total	246	294	540

[1] This question was asked only of Newark respondents.

17

Of those who never teach traditions but trust foreign language news programs, only 20 per cent have had U. S. schooling, while of those who teach traditions but trust American newscasts more, 34 per cent had had American schooling. In other words, American schooling is more likely to affect one's trust in newscasts than to affect the teaching of traditions.

In Table 15 one also notes a correlation between the carry-over of Old Country traditions and foreign language reading habits.

Table 15

READING FOREIGN LANGUAGE NEWSPAPERS
BY TEACHING OF OLD COUNTRY TRADITIONS
Among First and Second Generation Respondents

Teaches Old Country Traditions	Frequency of Reading		
	Often or sometimes	Never	Total
	No.	No.	No.
Often or sometimes	67	8	75
Never	48	64	112
Total	115	72	187*

* See footnote 2/, page 8.

The national groups are too small for further breakdown, but indications from the small sample are that the Jews and Germans constitute far more than their total sample proportion of those who never teach traditions but read foreign language papers. The greater distance in time of the German population from the old country and the lack of affections of Jews for the Russian traditions would account for this phenomenon.

There is even a positive correlation between the inculcation of traditions and the type of newspaper considered most reliable.

Table 16

MOST RELIABLE NEWSPAPER BY TEACHING OF OLD COUNTRY TRADITIONS
Among First and Second Generation Respondents

Teaches Old Country Traditions	Foreign Language	American	Total
	No.	No.	No.
Often or sometimes	135	178	313
Never	109	462	571
Total	244	640	884

Conclusions

1. Listening to shortwave is related to psychological nearness to the old country. Although more than 16 per cent of the entire sample of Poles, Italians, and Germans in Newark, Trenton, and Paterson, listen to shortwave from the old country, the first generation listen more than the second generation. The difference is striking when only those respondents are considered who have ready access to shortwave sets. Also, the Poles listen more than the Italians, the Italians more than the Germans.

2. Three-quarters of the first generation immigrants listen to local foreign language broadcasts and read foreign language newspapers.

3. By the second generation, interest in foreign language reading and listening decreases, being found in less than half of the sample.

4. Interest in foreign language newspapers decreases more sharply with the second generation than does interest in foreign language broadcasts. Several explanations may be advanced. In the first place, the radio can offer a broader field of interest than the newspaper and can include much entertainment. Moreover, it is apparent from the interviews that the spoken language carryover from one generation to another is more successful than the written. It is certainly true that reading difficulties have forced foreign language papers to devote more space to their English section.

5. There is decidedly more listening to foreign language programs and reading of foreign language newspapers than there is trust in them. This is true even among first generation immigrants who evidence more trust than the second generation.

6. These indices of communication seem to show that the Poles lag the most in the assimilation process; the Italians come next, then the Jews, and finally the Germans. Many of the Germans come to America before the members of the other groups. If only second generation contemporaries are considered, then the Jews have been Americanized most completely.

7. If the foreign language culture in the community is sufficiently concentrated, it tends to become self-sufficient, and a community of interests tends to form which is midway between the old country and the new. Thus the Italians seem to be so well organized that interest in and adaptation to the Italian-American community outweighs both the old country and the new. The Italian can and does rise in social and economic status within the Italian-American community, and so preserves his interest in and affection for it. The Jews show trends which are similar but complicated by the multiple culture of the Jew as compared to the Italian. Their lag in assimilation is a lag in dropping Jewish, not Russian culture. Thus their feelings toward radio and newspapers are decidedly different from the Italians. The other two groups studied here must make a considerable adjustment to the American community in order to rise in the world. This is particularly true of the Germans. These conclusions are drawn from the large studies of which this report is a part.

Appendix II

DESCRIPTION OF RESPONDENTS

Age

The mean ages of all first generation groups are about the same but the second generation Germans are on the average older than the second generation respondents of the other three groups.

Table 1.

AGE OF FIRST AND SECOND GENERATION RESPONDENTS*
by Nationality

Nationality	Mean Age in Years	
	First Generation	Second Generation
Poles	47	30
Italians	50	31
Russian Jews	47	30
Germans	50	41

* Newark respondents only

The obvious reason for the difference is the well-known fact that Germans were earlier immigrants to this country. Almost half of the German immigrants interviewed had come here before 1900, whereas only 20 per cent of the Italians, 9 per cent of the Jews, and 6 per cent of the Poles had done so. Second generation Germans would therefore be expected to be older. Another contributing factor is the tendency for second generation Germans to move from Newark to surrounding suburban towns.

That the average age of first generation Germans is not greater than that for the other nationalities can be explained by the bimodal wave of German immigration. Whereas almost half of the first generation Germans had come before 1900, there was also heavy concentration after 1920. The other three groups came in greatest force between 1900 and 1920.

Income

Of those who answered the questionnaire on family income, there is heavy concentration in the $1000-$2000 class. The Poles and Italians run considerably lower in income than the other two groups.

Education

In the first generation practically all had received some grammar school training. There is an increase in the amount of education in the second generation, but it is much less than might be expected: over half of each group had no more than grammar school education, except for the Jews of the second generation, among whom 75 per cent had been graduated from high school.

Occupation

The first generation Germans, Poles, and Italians generally fall into the laboring class, half of them skilled and half unskilled. A large number of Italians, however, own their own businesses. The second generation is preponderantly

in the skilled class. Some white collar and salespeople
make their appearance. Very few of the women work outside,
practically all falling in the housewife category. Unemployment is rife in all groups. Jews have a preponderance of
skilled labor, white collar, and salespeople, particularly in
the second generation, but also a considerable number of
shopkeepers.

APPENDIX III

The distribution of interviews in Newark, Trenton, and Paterson was based on 1930 census figures for the nationality groups studied. Since the survey was conducted some years after the census, the sample was altered according to the staff's knowledge of the current concentration of the several groups. For Jews, this was the sole determinant of the samples because the census does not distinguish them as such.

Enumerators made no more than two interviews on a block except in densely populated areas. Although it might be faulty in some ways, we think the sample representative of both neighborhood and economic groupings.

OCCUPATIONAL CLASSIFICATION OF ITALIAN RESPONDENTS
FOR THOSE ANSWERING SPECIFICALLY

MALE

GENERATION	FIRST	SECOND	THIRD	MIXED
ARCHITECT	-	1	-	-
ARTIST	-	-	-	1
APPRENTICE-EMBALMER	1	-	-	-
AUTO-MECHANIC	-	2	-	-
ASBESTOS-MECHANIC	-	1	-	-
BARBER	18	4	-	-
BRASS-WORKER	1	-	-	-
BOSS-PLUMBER	1	-	-	-
BARTENDER	1	3	-	-
BOARD OF HEALTH	-	1	-	-
BAKER	2	1	-	-
BUS-DRIVER	1	1	-	-
BOXING-INSTRUCTOR	-	1	-	-
BUTCHER	-	2	-	-
CARPENTER	5	1	-	-
CLOCK-MAKER	1	-	-	-
COLOR-MATCHER	1	-	-	-
CUTTER	1	-	-	-
COUNTERMAN	-	1	-	-
CLERK	-	1	-	-
CITY-FIREMAN	-	-	1	-
DRUGGIST	4	1	-	-
DRAFTSMAN	-	1	-	-
ENGRAVER	-	1	-	-
FURRIER	1	-	-	-
FOREMAN	-	-	1	-
FACTORY	-	1	-	-
GARAGE-HELPER	-	1	-	-
GROCERY-CLERK	-	1	-	-
GOVERNMENT-PENSION	1	-	-	-
HOUSEWIFE	-	1	-	-
HOD-CARRIER	1	-	-	-
ICEMAN	1	-	-	-
IRONWORKER	-	1	-	-
JANITOR	1	-	-	-
JEWELER	-	1	-	-
LABORER	10	3	-	-
LEATHER-WORKER	1	-	-	-
LINOLEUM-WORKER	2	-	-	-
MASON	4	2	-	-
MANAGER	-	1	-	-
MECHANIC	-	1	-	1
MECH. INSPECTOR	-	1	-	-
MUSICIAN	-	1	-	-
MERCHANT	-	1	-	-

MALE

GENERATION	FIRST	SECOND	THIRD	MIXED
MALE CLERK	1	-	-	-
MACHINIST	1	-	-	-
NO ANSWER	1	-	-	-
NONE	6	1	-	-
OWN BUSINESS	4	1	-	-
OIL-SETTER	-	-	-	1
PEDDLER	2	-	-	-
PAINTER	1	4	-	-
POST-OFFICE-CLERK	-	2	1	-
PAINTER & DECORATOR	-	2	-	-
PLATFORM-LOADER	-	1	-	-
PRESS OPERATOR	-	1	-	-
POSTAL-CLERK	-	1	-	-
PLATER	-	-	1	-
RELIEF	1	-	-	1
RESTAURANT OWNER	-	1	-	-
RIDING ACADEMY	-	1	-	-
ROUTE-SALESMAN	-	-	1	-
RETIRED	11	-	-	-
SOCIAL-WORKER	-	1	-	-
SALESMAN	1	5	1	-
STORE-CLERK	-	2	-	-
SERVICE-STATION-OPERATOR	-	4	-	-
STUDENT	-	1	-	-
SHOEMAKER	12	-	-	-
STONECUTTER	1	-	-	-
STOREKEEPER	1	-	-	-
TAILOR	8	3	-	-
TRUCK-DRIVER	-	1	-	-
TEXTILE-FINISHER	-	-	-	1
TRUCKMAN	3	-	-	-
TILE MECHANIC	1	-	-	-
UNEMPLOYED	31	45	3	3
WRAPPER	-	1	-	-
WIRE-MAILER	-	1	-	-
WHITE WASHER	-	1	-	-
W.P.A.	6	1	-	-
WATCHMAN	1	-	-	-
TOTAL	152	118	9	8

The sample of 28.7 obtained on this question may appear too small for reliable interpretation. However, it represents what the staff believed to be an adequate cross-section.

Appendix V

ITALIAN PROFESSIONAL MEN

PROFESSIONS	1922	1925	1930	1935	1939
ACCOUNTING FIRMS	-	1	1	2	2
ARCHITECTURAL FIRMS	10	11	9	5	4
CHIROPRACTORS	-	-	-	2	2
DENTISTS	2	9	13	26	36
DRUG STORES	28	41	39	40	32
LEGAL FIRMS	36	58	72	97	112
PHYSICIANS & SURGEONS	33	50	28	85	107
TOTALS	109	170	162	257	295

PLACE	UNEMPLOYABLE N. J. Relief Census 1937			
	POLES	RUSSIANS	HUNGARIAN	GERMANS
STATE OF NEW JERSEY	505 / 23.4	314 / 34.2	193 / 34.8	392 / 47.1
COUNTY OF ESSEX	116 / 27.0	151 / 36.1	27 / 40.9	89 / 49.4
CITY OF NEWARK	104 / 26.4	142 / 35.8	24 / 40.7	71 / 50.0
JERSEY CITY	61 / 16.3	13 / 23.2	3 / 27.3	41 / 38.3
TRENTON	31 / 36.5	7 / 41.1	25 / 35.7	14 / 56.0
CAMDEN	13 / 19.1	9 / 42.8	- / -	10 / 43.5
PATERSON	27 / 23.3	6 / 25.0	4 / 57.1	10 / 33.3
ELIZABETH	15 / 48.4	8 / 40.0	5 / 100.0	4 / 66.7

REFERS TO NUMBER OF UNEMPLOYABLE COMPARED
WITH TOTAL ON RELIEF FOR EACH NATIONAL
GROUP FOR COMMUNITY IN QUESTION

TABLE SHOWING THE INCIDENCE OF DOMESTIC
RELATIONS COURT CASES FOR LEADING ETHNIC GROUPS

NATIONALITY	Total in Essex County 1930 ***	% of Total Essex County 1930	DOMESTIC RELATIONS COURT CASES*					
			Court Cases in 1928	% of Total Court Case 1928	Court Cases in 1933	% of Total Court Case 1933	Court Cases in 1938	% of Total Court Cases 1938
Italian	125,865	15.1	123	19.5	209	18.0	177	18.1
Jewish**	77,000	9.3	78	11.4	140	10.8	85	8.7
German	125,174	15.0	90	14.1	154	11.8	102	10.4
Polish	23,683	2.8	44	6.9	79	6.1	69	7.1
Ukrainians	10,000	1.2	0	.0	12	0.9	4	0.4
Negroes	60,236	7.2	27	4.2	129	10.1	96	9.8
Irish	76,114	9.1	186	21.5	122	9.4	120	12.3
Others	335,441	40.3	146	22.8	455	34.9	324	33.2
Totals	833,513	100.0	839	100.0	1,298	100.0	977	100.0

*   From Domestic Relation Court Records
** Estimated from Jewish Census 1927
*** County of which Newark is the metropolis.

Appendix VIII(

NATIONALITY OF COUNCILMEN CITY OF NEWARK
1891 to 1917

(Italian, Jewish, Irish and German Councilmen)

YEAR	ITALIANS	JEWS	GERMANS	IRISH
1891	None	None	13	16
1892	None	1	12	16
1893	None	1	9	12
1894	None	1	5	11
1895	None	7	11	10
1896	None	8	12	10
1897	1	4	11	11
1898	1	3	12	14
1899	None	4	13	13
1900	1	2	13	13
1901	None	3	12	15
1902	None	3	13	14
1903	None	1	15	14
1904	1	1	12	16
1905	1	1	13	14
1906	2	1	14	13
1907	2	3	11	14
1908	2	3	10	15
1909	None	2	14	16
1910	None	1	15	16
1911	1	3	11	17
1912	1	3	8	18
1913	1	3	8	20
1914	1	4	10	16
1915	2	5	8	14
1916	2	4	7	18
1917	2	4	9	17
TOTAL	21	76	301	393

CANDIDATES ELECTED TO THE CITY OF NEWARK
1917 - 1927
(JEWISH, ITALIAN, GERMAN, IRISH birth or extraction)

YEAR	ITALIAN	JEWISH	GERMAN	IRISH
1917	None	None	None	Chas. P. Gillen John F. Monohan Wm. J. Brennan
1921	None	None	F. C. Breidenbach	Chas. P. Gillen Wm. J. Brennan
1922				John Howe replaced T. Raymond who died
1925	None	None	F. C. Breidenbach	John F. Murray John Howe Chas. P. Gillen Wm. J. Brennan
1929	None	None	None	John Howe John F. Murray Chas. P. Gillen Wm. Brennan
1930				Brennan died Wm. J. Eagen filled unexpired term
1932		Meyer C. Ellen- stein chosen to fill unexpired term left vacant by death of John F. Murray		
1933	Anthony F. Minisi	Meyer C. Ellen- stein	None	Michael P. Duffy Reginald R. Parnell
1937	None	Meyer C. Ellen- stein	None	Vincent J. Murphy Joseph Byrne, Jr. Michael Duffy (now deceased)

Appendix X

TYPE OF ORGANIZATION
TO WHICH ITALIANS BELONG

Generation	1st	2nd
Social	9	3
Political	4	3
Educational	0	3
Trade Union	21	15
Religious	32	13
Service & Business	3	7
Fraternal	36	15
Athletic	2	12
Nationality	16	5
Other	4	6
No Answer	270	224
Total Answers	127	107
Grand Total	397	331

Appendix XI

Wards of Respondents

First Generation		Second Generation	
1 -	95	1 -	85
2 -	2	2 -	5
3 -		3 -	
4 -		4 -	
5 -	30	5 -	27
6 -	26	6 -	14
7 -		7 -	
8 -	51	8 -	32
9 -	4	9 -	1
10 -	11	10 -	10
11 -	24	11 -	19
12 -	1	12 -	
13 -	28	13 -	29
14 -	96	14 -	39
15 -	8	15 -	3
16 -		16 -	3
	376		267

Provinces of Origin in Italy of Respondents

First Generation		Second Generation
32	Abruzzi and Molise	15
10	Apulia	1
6	Basilicata	11
10	Calabria	12
177	Campania	137
2	Liguria	2
2	Lombardia	2
4	Piedmont	
13	Roma	6
69	Sicilia	36
3	Tuscany	1
10	Venetia	3
1	Sardinia	1
338		227

BIBLIOGRAPHY

Bogardus, Emory S. Immigration and Race Attitudes. Boston, D.C. Heath, 1928.

Budge, E.A. Wallis, Amulets and Superstitions. New York, Oxford University Press, 1930.

Clark, Francis. Our Italian Fellow Citizens in Their Old Homes and Their New. New York, Small, Maynard and Co., 1919.

D'Angleo, Pascal. Son of Italy. New York, Macmillan Co., 1924.

Foerster, Robert. Italian Emigration of Our Times. Cambridge, Mass., Harvard University Press, 1924.

Franchetti, Leopoldo, and Sonnino, Sidney S. La Sicilia nel 1876. Firenze, Valleche, 1877.

Greenfield, Kent. Economics and Liberalism in the Risorgimento. Baltimore, Johns Hopkins Press, 1934.

Huntington, Ellsworth. Climatic Change and Agricultural Exhaustion as Elements in the Fall of Rome. (In the Quarterly Journal of Economics, v.31, pp.173-208, February, 1917).

Irwin, Grace. Michelangelo in Newark. (In Harper's Monthly, v.143, pp.446-454, September 1921).

Italy. Administero di Agricultura, Industria et Commercio. Censimento, 1900. Rome, 1901.

Italy. Commissariato dell' Emigrazione. Probizione dello Sbarco negli Stati Uniti agli Stranieri analfabeti. (Bollatin Emigrazione Anno 1915, Nos. 10-12. Rome, 1916).

Italy. Commissariato dell' Emigrazione. Rendiconti delle Sedute nell' Anno 1904. (Bolletino Emigrazione, Anno 1904, No.10, Rome, 1905).

Italy. Commissariato dell' Emigrazione. Rendiconti delle Sadute del Coniglio dell Emigrazione Seunte nell' Anno 1903. (Bolletino Emigrazione Anno 1904, No.9 Rome, 1905).

Italy. Parlamento. Atti della Giunta per la Inchiesta Agraria e sulle Condizioni delle Classi Agricole. Rome, 1879-1884. 15 vols.

Italy. Parlamento. Inchiesta Parlamentare sulle Condizioni dei Contadini nelle Provincie Meridionali e nella Sicilia. Rome, 1909-1911. 8 vols.

Italy. Parlamento. Risultati dell' Inchiesta sulle Condizioni Igieniche e Sanitarie nei Comuni del Regno: Relazione Generale. Rome, 1886.

King, Bolton and Okey,Thomas. Italy Today. New York, Charles Scribner's and Sons, 1913.

Lazarsfeld, Paul F. Radio and the Printed Page. Duell, Sloan and Pearse, 1940.

Mangano, Antonio. Sons of Italy. New York, Missionary Education Movement, 1917.

Mariano, John Horace. The Italian Contribution to American Democracy. Boston, Christopher Publishing House, 1921.

New Jersey, Labor Department. Bureau of Statistics and Records. Manufacturers' Industrial Directory of New Jersey, 1939. Trenton, 1940.

Odencrants, Louise C. Italian Women in Industry. New York, Russell Sage Foundation, 1919.

Sartorio, Enrico C. Social and Religious Life of the Italian in America. Boston, Christopher Publishing House, 1918.

Schiavo, Giovanni. Italians in America Before the Civil War. New York, Vijo Press, 1934.

Titoni,Tommaso. Italy's Foreign and Colonial Policy. New York, E.P. Dutton and Co., 1914.

Williams, Phyllis. South Italian Folkways. New Haven, Conn., Yale University Press, 1938.

The Italian American Experience

An Arno Press Collection

Angelo, Valenti. **Golden Gate.** 1939

Assimilation of the Italian Immigrant. 1975

Bohme, Frederick G. **A History of the Italians in New Mexico.** (Doctoral Dissertation, The University of New Mexico, 1958). 1975

Boissevain, Jeremy. **The Italians of Montreal:** Social Adjustment in a Plural Society. 1971

Churchill, Charles W. **The Italians of Newark:** A Community Study. (Doctoral Thesis, New York University, 1942). 1975

Clark, Francis E. **Our Italian Fellow Citizens in Their Old Homes and Their New.** 1919

D'Agostino, Guido. **Olives on the Apple Tree.** 1940

D'Angelo, Pascal. **Son of Italy.** 1924

Fenton, Edwin. **Immigrants and Unions,** A Case Study: Italians and American Labor, 1870-1920. (Doctoral Thesis, Harvard University, 1957). 1975

Forgione, Louis. **The River Between.** 1928

Fucilla, Joseph G. **The Teaching of Italian in the United States:** A Documentary History. 1967

Garlick, Richard C., Jr. et al. **Italy and Italians in Washington's Time.** 1933

Giovannitti, Arturo. **The Collected Poems of Arturo Giovannitti.** 1962

Istituto di Studi Americani, Università degli Studi di Firenze (Institute of American Studies, University of Florence). **Gli Italiani negli Stati Uniti** (Italians in the United States). 1972

Italians in the City: Health and Related Social Needs. 1975

Italians in the United States: A Repository of Rare Tracts and Miscellanea. 1975

Lapolla, Garibaldi M. **The Fire in the Flesh.** 1931

Lapolla, Garibaldi M. **The Grand Gennaro.** 1935

Mariano, John Horace. **The Italian Contribution to American Democracy.** 1922

Mariano, John H[orace]. **The Italian Immigrant and Our Courts.** 1925

Pagano, Jo. **Golden Wedding.** 1943

Parenti, Michael John. **Ethnic and Political Attitudes:** A Depth Study of Italian Americans. (Doctoral Dissertation, Yale University, 1962). 1975

Protestant Evangelism Among Italians in America. 1975

Radin, Paul. **The Italians of San Francisco:** Their Adjustment and Acculturation. Parts I and II. 1935

Rose, Philip M. **The Italians in America.** 1922

Ruddy, Anna C. (Christian McLeod, pseud.). **The Heart .of the Stranger:** A Story of Little Italy. 1908

Schiavo, Giovanni Ermenegildo. **Italian-American History:** Volume I. 1947

Schiavo, Giovanni [Ermenegildo]. **Italian-American History:** The Italian Contribution to the Catholic Church in America. Volume II. 1949

Schiavo, Giovanni [Ermenegildo]. **The Italians in America Before the Civil War.** 1934

Schiavo, Giovanni E[rmenegildo]. **The Italians in Chicago:** A Study in Americanization. 1928

Schiavo, Giovanni [Ermenegildo]. **The Italians in Missouri.** 1929

Schiro, George. **Americans by Choice:** History of the Italians in Utica. 1940

La Società Italiana di Fronte Alle Prime Migrazioni di Massa. (Italian Society at the Beginnings of the Mass Migrations). New Foreword (in English) by Francesco Cordasco. 1968

Speranza, Gino. **Race or Nation:** A Conflict of Divided Loyalties. 1925

Stella, Antonio. **Some Aspects of Italian Immigration to the United States:** Statistical Data and General Considerations Based Chiefly Upon the United States Censuses and Other Official Publications. 1924

Ulin, Richard Otis. **The Italo-American Student in the American Public School:** A Description and Analysis of Differential Behavior. (Doctoral Thesis, Harvard University, 1958). 1975

Valletta, Clement Lawrence. **A Study of Americanization in Carneta:** Italian-American Identity Through Three Generations. (Doctoral Dissertation, University of Pennsylvania, 1968). 1975

Villari, Luigi. **Gli Stati Uniti d'America e l'Emigrazione Italiana.** (The United States and Italian Immigration). 1912

Workers of the Writers' Program. Work Projects Administration in the State of Nebraska. **The Italians of Omaha.** 1941